LIVING BEYOND YOUR DREAMS

11 PRINCIPLES FOR TRIUMPHING IN LIFE AND LEADERSHIP

WILLIAM J. FERGUSON

Post Hill PRESS

A POST HILL PRESS BOOK
ISBN: 979-8-88845-546-3
ISBN (eBook): 979-8-88845-547-0

Living Beyond Your Dreams:
11 Principles for Triumphing in Life and Leadership
© 2025 by William J. Ferguson
All Rights Reserved

Cover design by Cody Corcoran

This book, as well as any other Post Hill Press publications, may be purchased in bulk quantities at a special discounted rate. Contact orders@posthillpress.com for more information.

This is a work of nonfiction. All people, locations, events, and situations are portrayed to the best of the author's memory.

Post Hill Press
New York • Nashville
posthillpress.com

Published in the United States of America
1 2 3 4 5 6 7 8 9 10

Advance Praise for Living Beyond Your Dreams

"*Living Beyond Your Dreams* is packed with helpful principles and inspiring stories about success in business and in life. Bill's thoughtful insights embody one of his core principles of 'Giving Generously,' which he does to the benefit of his readers on each and every page so that they can live beyond their dreams."

> —JOHN HOPE BRYANT, founder, chairman, and CEO of Operation HOPE, serial entrepreneur, and author

"*Living Beyond Your Dreams* reflects Bill Ferguson's heart for creating change in an industry that desperately needs change and offers an inspirational roadmap for making that change a reality. Any corporation can leverage the book's insights to create an inclusive culture that will impact organizational performance."

> —LESLIE D. HALE, president and chief executive officer, RLJ Lodging Trust; board member, Delta Airlines; trustee, Howard University

"After over four decades in senior management recruiting, Bill Ferguson shares invaluable insights that have propelled hundreds of his clients to extraordinary success. The key takeaway: You must become the CEO of your own self before you can lead others. *Living Beyond Your Dreams* distills the essential principles identified by Bill that aspiring leaders should consider cultivating within themselves to achieve success and effect positive change in the world. It is a powerful treatise written by someone who has borne witness to those who have lived their dreams."

> —M. BRIAN BLAKE, president, Georgia State University

To my wife, Penny, who unselfishly sacrificed the bandwidth needed for me to embark upon this remarkable journey. And to everyone else with a passion for living beyond their dreams.

I am dedicating this book (and its profits) to my foundation, The Ferguson Centers for Leadership Excellence, and our leadership team, whose unfailing commitment to recruiting diverse college students into our industry is simply remarkable! Providing these future leaders access to the C-suite and boardroom is the best way not only to enhance corporate performance but also to address this country's growing economic divide.

CONTENTS

WHEN OPPORTUNITY KNOCKS

It was 2016 and I was happily minding my own business, which is to say I was minding the business of RLJ Lodging Trust as its president, CEO, and director.

The legendary Bob Johnson and I co-founded RLJ Development in 2000, and we took it public as RLJ Lodging Trust in 2011. In addition to a dream partner, I had a dream team around me. It was a dream job, and I had no plans to leave.

Then Bill Ferguson entered my life.

When Bill comes calling, I can assure you that opportunity is always knocking.

In this case, Blackstone and Hilton Hotels had hired Bill's firm to identify and recruit a CEO for a new real estate investment trust in the lodging and hospitality sector. Blackstone, the world's largest alternative asset manager, was backing the deal with capital, and Hilton was contributing assets in the form of sixty-seven high-end hotel properties.

Blackstone and Hilton wanted a CEO with experience managing a lodging REIT and who had the investor credibility to lead a successful IPO. Bill identified me as a candidate, and we discussed the opportunity over dinner. He wanted to confirm that I would be a fit, and I wanted to find out why I would leave the comfort of RLJ Lodging Trust for something different.

This wasn't a case where Bill was asking me to simply trade one CEO role for another. I had worked for Hilton earlier in my career, and in fact, RLJ Development was a spin-off of Hilton properties. I not only knew Jon Gray at Blackstone and Chris Nassetta at Hilton well, but I trusted and respected them. I was drawn to their vision for the business, liked the idea of taking on a fresh challenge, and had a more than capable team in place to carry on the work at RLJ. Leslie Hale, also profiled in this book, eventually became CEO at RLJ, a role she is in today!

So as hard as it was to leave Bob Johnson and my team at RLJ, I agreed to take the role as CEO (and now chairman) of the newly created Park Hotels & Resorts (NYSE: PK).

During the process, Bill and I became friends, and my respect for him as a leader and industry advocate grew. I am confident he's the perfect person to write this book, and I believe *Living Beyond Your Dreams* will be a powerful force in enhancing diversity across the leadership ranks of our industry.

Bill and I spent a great deal of time together when he was vetting CEO candidates for Park Hotels & Resorts, so he learned my story and background, and I got to know him as well. He then helped me identify and recruit our board, which included the likes of retired Continental Airlines CEO Gordon Bethune, former Saks CEO Stephen Sadove, former US Senator Joe Lieberman, and former Weyerhaeuser CFO Patricia Bedient. Bill also played a role in recruiting some members of my leadership team.

It became clear that Bill takes a strategic and merit-based approach to recruiting leaders and board members. He looks for the people who have the right skills, who are the right fit, and who can bring diverse backgrounds and experiences that yield fresh and innovative insights.

He also knows there's a lack of diversity in the leadership pipeline across real estate and hospitality firms, and he has a passion for doing something about it. This book represents that passion.

Bill interviewed twenty-four executives, including me, who can speak to the trials and tribulations of rising from humble beginnings to become leaders, typically CEOs! And while this book addresses the major barriers my colleagues and I often faced along the way, he takes a decidedly optimistic approach that will encourage and equip anyone who reads these stories.

The thing I appreciate about Bill and that shines through in this book is the way he puts actions behind his conviction that a diverse culture leads to superior corporate performance. This isn't just something he talks about with friends. He's creating positive change by putting his time and money where his mouth is.

In his foundation's work with colleges that are rich in ethnic diversity, The Ferguson Centers for Leadership Excellence is doing things no one else in the industry is doing. They provide students with tuition assistance, offer holistic mentoring and counseling that helps students work through challenges and determine the best career path in the industry, and source summer full-time jobs for students.

Bill has a conviction to help students develop an interest in the real estate and hospitality industry, to find their fit in the industry, to stick with and do well in college when others tempt them to abandon their dreams, and to succeed in their professional careers once they graduate.

This book plays a role in Bill's strategy because it offers hope and direction, not only for students but for anyone working their way through the often treacherous waters of the corporate world. Furthermore, it offers insights and direction to leaders like me—leaders who are in a position to hire and groom the next generation of executives.

With this book, Bill is calling us all to live beyond our dreams. And when Bill comes calling, opportunity knocks. Open the door, or in this case the book, and discover how you can live beyond your dreams.

—Thomas J. Baltimore Jr., chairman and CEO,
Park Hotels & Resorts

BUILDING ON ARNE'S LEGACY

Arne Sorenson knew that my work required a great deal of travel and that I frequently stayed in hotels that were part of the Marriott brand, so he often sought my feedback on those experiences.

"When you go to one of our hotels," he would tell me, "please text me with what you liked and what you didn't like."

As the president and CEO of Marriott International Inc., Arne cared deeply about the company, its assets, and most of all, the people—those who worked for the company and the guests who stayed in their hotels and resorts. So he never wanted to find himself isolated in the ivory towers of C-suite leadership, where crunched numbers can drive decisions with no connection to the lives those decisions impact (even in the hospitality industry).

Instead, he actively sought information and insights that helped him know and understand what employees and guests were experiencing, why they were experiencing it, how they could build on what was good, and how they could improve what wasn't.

It was that attitude, I believe, that made Arne not only successful but beloved by those who knew him. He was a leader who cared, he was a leader who served, and therefore, he was a leader who left a legacy.

Like others who knew him and knew of his battle with pancreatic cancer, I was stung by the news in 2021 that Arne had died at the age of sixty-two. I knew Arne because of our mutual business interests, but I also considered him a dear and personal friend. And not long after his death—just as I began to transition out of my full-time role as CEO of the company I founded—Arne's life, leadership, and legacy helped inspire the next phase in my journey, which includes this book.

My conversations with Arne over the years often turned to the remarkable story of his success with Marriott. It wasn't something he brought up, but I would ask questions about it because I found it fascinating and inspiring.

Arne shepherded Marriott's $13 billion acquisition of Starwood Hotels and Resorts, led the company's move into home rentals, and was an outspoken advocate when it came to sustainability, human rights, and inclusion issues. Under his leadership, in fact, Marriott was number one on DiversityInc's Top 50 Companies for Diversity list in 2020[1] and became the first hospitality company named to DiversityInc's Hall of Fame.[2]

But it wasn't just the results that grabbed my attention, although those were significant. More interesting to me was the how and the why of his leadership journey.

Arne, just the third CEO in Marriott's history and the first without the family's surname, didn't come from a wealthy family of business icons or entrepreneurs. He was born in Tokyo, where his father was a pastor and missionary for the Lutheran Church. When the family moved back to Minnesota, his mother taught school and Arnie grew up on a healthy diet

---

1   "Marriott International Ranks #1 On DiversityInc Top 50 List," Marriott News Center, May 6, 2020, https://news.marriott.com/news/2020/05/06/marriott-international-ranks-1-on-diversityinc-top-50-list.

2   "Marriott International Named to DiversityInc Hall of Fame," Marriott News Center, May 7, 2021, https://news.marriott.com/news/2021/05/07/marriott-international-named-to-diversityinc-hall-of-fame.

of midwestern values. He also remained active in his faith, attending Luther College in Iowa (where he met his wife) and taking summer mission trips to places like Beirut.

Given that background, Arne easily could have taken his undergraduate degrees in business and religion and followed his father into the ministry, his mother into education, or worked in some service-related field in the nonprofit sector. Instead, Arne went to law school and then joined Latham & Watkins, one of the largest and most powerful law firms in the world. He specialized in mergers and acquisitions, rose to become a partner with the firm, and eventually joined Marriott in 1996 as associate general counsel before ascending to his role as CEO.

In short, Arnie Sorenson, the son of a pastor and a schoolteacher, became a high-powered attorney who specialized in the cutthroat field of mergers and acquisitions. Even though he had no background in finance, he became Marriott's chief financial officer. And even though he had never worked in—much less run—a hotel, he became Marriott's chief operations officer.

As president and CEO, Arne became known for his strategic foresight, but the pastor and teacher influences never left him, because he also was known for his incredible humility and humanity. And never was that humanity on greater display than in a video message he delivered to Marriott's workforce on March 20, 2020.

With the pandemic still in its early stages and the hospitality industry reeling, Arne compassionately talked through the realities of the situation and the tough decisions the company's leaders were making to ensure Marriott's survival. The chemotherapy from his cancer treatments had left him bald—a new look many had not seen before the video—but he made it clear he was focused on their shared crisis, not his personal problems.

He talked about a hiring freeze, staff reductions, and limits on how their properties would operate during the crisis.

And since it was a shared crisis, he announced that he and Bill Marriott, the company's executive chairman, would not take a salary for the remainder of 2020 and that the other top executives were taking a 50 percent cut in pay.

Near the end of the message, Arne's eyes welled with tears and he fought off his emotions.

"As a leader, I have experienced so many wonderful highs, and a good number of challenging lows," he said. "I can tell you that I have never had a more difficult moment than this one. There is simply nothing worse than telling highly valued associates, people who are the very heart of this company, that their roles are being impacted by events completely outside of their control."[3]

Arne was smart, strategic, and tough, but he also genuinely cared about people, and his belief in helping others extended far beyond his Marriott family. To honor that legacy, the Marriott Foundation created a $20 million endowment to establish the Marriott-Sorenson Center for Hospitality Leadership at Howard University, one of the top-ranked historically Black colleges and universities (HBCUs) in America. Marriott International also donated $1 million to support the new center's programs.

"Arne's passion for creating a culture of opportunity brought real change in the executive ranks of our company," Bill Marriott said when the center was announced a few weeks after Arne died. "But work remains to be done. Our industry needs a pipeline of diverse leadership talent and that's exactly what this center will achieve."[4]

---

3   Arne Sorenson, "COVID-19: A Message to Marriott International Associates from President and CEO Arne Sorenson," filmed March 20, 2020, video, 4:41, https://youtu.be/SprFgoU6aO0?si=QCzBgS3Fj0C_oRKi.

4   "The J. Willard and Alice S. Marriott Foundation Announces $20 Million Endowment at Howard University to Establish the Marriott-Sorenson Center for Hospitality Leadership," Marriott International News Center, February 24, 2021, https://news.marriott.com/news/2021/02/24/the-j-willard-and-alice-s-marriott-foundation-announces-20-million-endowment-at-howard-university-to-establish-the-marriott-sorenson-center-for-hospitality-leadership.

Because much of my life's work has involved working with leaders in real estate–related sectors, including the hospitality industry, I have seen firsthand the need for training and equipping the leaders of tomorrow. In fact, the idea behind my first book, *Keepers of the Castle*, was to survey the industry landscape and unpack the key attributes top executives needed for guiding their businesses through the ever-changing market.

That book, published on the heels of the Great Recession in 2009, underscored the importance of some fundamental leadership principles that have remained as applicable as ever. But even as the industry and market have continued to morph like the skylines across America, one thing has changed little: The leaders at the top of most corporations, and especially across our industry sector, remain, like me, white and male.

Overall, corporate America has made progress in this area in recent years. In 1980, every CEO of a company in the top fifty of the Fortune 500 was a white male, and a decade later there was only one non-white male in that group—a Middle Eastern male. In 2000, a white female and a Black male joined the list. And there were four non-white male CEOs of top fifty companies in 2010. In 2023, however, there were thirteen non-white, non-male CEOs of Fortune 50 companies—six white females, one South Asian female, one Black male, one Latino male, three South Asian males, and one Latina female.[5]

Only one of those led a company in a real estate–related field—Priscilla Almodovar, currently CEO of Fannie Mae, who formerly led real estate businesses for JPMorgan Chase and has spent much of her career in roles related to affordable housing.

For example, if we look specifically at real estate investment trusts (REITs), the top ten (by market cap) had three non-white CEOs, but all three of those were men—Prologis

---

5   "The Diversity of the Top 50 Fortune 500 CEOs Over Time," QualtricsXM, August 4, 2023, https://www.qualtrics.com/blog/fortune-500-ceo-diversity/.

(Hamid Moghadam), Welltower (Shankh Mitra), and Realty Income (Sumit Roy).[6]

The problem, as Arne and the Marriott family knew, is that we have a fundamental need to increase opportunities for diverse leaders to make their way into the upper echelons of corporate America. Too often college students don't realize the career options in real estate–related sectors, and many of the top leaders in those sectors, quite frankly, aren't doing enough to cultivate the type of diverse talent that can give their companies a competitive advantage.

Make no mistake: Inclusive leadership is good for business, and research confirms this reality. In a 2019 article for the *Harvard Business Review*, Juliet Bourke and Andrea Titus noted that "teams with inclusive leaders are 17 percent more likely to report that they are high performing, 20 percent more likely to say they make high-quality decisions, and 29 percent more likely to report behaving collaboratively." They also found a correlation between "perceptions of inclusion" and a reduction in absenteeism.[7]

McKinsey, meanwhile, has researched the business case for diversity since 2014 and found that "the relationship between diversity on executive teams and the likelihood of financial outperformance has strengthened over time."[8]

All too often, however, women and people of color are steered toward roles in human resources—roles that are

---

6   Marcus Lu, "The World's Largest Real Estate Investment Trusts (REITs)," Visual Capitalist, April 7, 2022, https://www.visualcapitalist.com/the-worlds-largest-real-estate-investment-trusts-reits/.

7   Juliet Bourke and Andrea Titus, "Why Inclusive Leaders Are Good for Organizations, and How to Become One," *Harvard Business Review*, March 29, 2019, https://hbr.org/2019/03/why-inclusive-leaders-are-good-for-organizations-and-how-to-become-one.

8   Sundiatu Dixon-Fyle, Kevin Dolan, Dame Vivian Hunt, and Sara Prince, "Diversity Wins: How Inclusion Matters," McKinsey & Company, May 19, 2020, https://www.mckinsey.com/featured-insights/diversity-and-inclusion/diversity-wins-how-inclusion-matters.

important, mind you, but that typically aren't as likely to be an on-ramp to become a CEO.

This must change, but the answer isn't as simple as promoting more women and people of color into executive-level roles in any industry, including real estate. As Gil Borok, CEO of Colliers, pointed out, we also need to create a bigger pipeline of talent and prepare them for top roles.

"There's a long history of why this industry has been white male dominated," Borok said in a 2023 interview with *Commercial Observer*. "All of the firms, even the smaller firms, are making significant strides to try and diversify their populations on every metric. But the number of qualified people to do that doesn't exist in a way that can get us to a meaningful percentage in the near term."[9]

It's also problematic that many commercial real estate firms only recruit from one or two top colleges. They have relationships with those universities, and they like the talent they produce, but those schools typically lack diversity and therefore feed the industry with a lack of diversity.

Reggie Samuel, founder and managing director of the Leumas Group, a privately held real estate management firm in Virginia, used a fishing analogy to describe the reality.

"Too frequently we feel that Black talent is too hard to find," Samuel, who is Black, said in a 2020 article for *Commercial Property Executive*. "I think the problem is that we're all fishing for freshwater bass using saltwater tackle."[10]

9   Celia Young, "After Three Years of Promises Is CRE Any More Diverse?" *Commercial Observer*, February 27, 2023, https://commercialobserver. com/2023/02/is-commercial-real-estate-more-diverse-after-years-of-promises/.

10 Holly Dutton, "Real Estate Has a Diversity Problem. Will This Moment Lead to Real Change?" *Commercial Property Executive*, August 3, 2020. https://www. commercialsearch.com/news/keeping-the-momentum-furthering-diversity-in-cre/.

I don't know about the bait, but I do believe we can improve the waters in which our industry fishes for talent. So just as Arne had inspired me personally as a leader, the Marriott-Sorenson Center for Hospitality Leadership inspired me to take action that I hope will create a positive change when it comes to diversity in leadership.

In addition to supporting their efforts, I launched the Ferguson Charitable Foundation in 2023, and from it The Ferguson Centers for Leadership Excellence. Using the partnership at Howard as a blueprint, our program expands the concept by working with colleges rich in ethnic diversity, including multiple HBCUs, and promoting careers more broadly across all real estate–related industries.

The Ferguson Centers for Leadership Excellence already has seventy-five fellows working on undergraduate minors in real estate–related disciplines at twenty-five colleges, and the hope is to equip and inspire these next-generation leaders for C-suite careers in relevant sectors.

When I began to share my passion for this cause, friends suggested I write a book that complements the message. So the original idea for *Living Beyond Your Dreams* was to interview successful industry leaders who are women and/or people of color about the barriers they faced in their journeys and how they overcame them. For college students, leaders early in their professional journey, and companies trying to mentor and develop diverse talent, I felt the stories would provide inspiration and practical wisdom for navigating their careers.

That idea morphed as my research progressed. As you'll see, rather than building the framework of the book around the barriers, my team and I found the practical principles the leaders shared were far more enlightening, inspiring, and useful.

There were many principles, of course, but we narrowed them to what we saw as the eleven most relevant for improving the odds of an emerging leader's success in the face of some undeniable barriers.

I interviewed twenty-four leaders from a variety of sectors, including the previously mentioned Priscilla Almodovar and Sumit Roy. All have achieved incredible success, all have overcome barriers, and all have lived beyond their dreams. In that respect, they all have something in common with Arne, who not only lived beyond his dreams but inspired others to do so as well.

Everyone faces barriers on the path to success; some just face more than others. But regardless of the barriers you face and the unique journey you are on, I believe the principles shared in this book demonstrate the proven firepower for living beyond your dreams.

Part I

DARE TO DREAM

Alice Carr showed up for an interview at UCLA's law school with an unusual goal in mind: "I was hoping they were going to talk me into being a lawyer," she told me.

It was the early 1990s, and Alice had recently graduated Phi Beta Kappa from Occidental College, a small liberal arts school in the heart of Los Angeles. Her agenda at Occidental had consisted mainly of soaking in all that she could experience and learn, and she left with degrees in American studies and German literature. Alice had a lot of interests and passions, but her path wasn't clear yet.

She was smart, articulate, persuasive, and had a passion for social justice long before the term was in vogue, so a career as a public interest attorney arose as the most logical option and she began applying to law schools.

In the meantime, she took a job as a paralegal for a law firm in Los Angeles and quickly mastered the skills of the job, most of which hadn't been part of her college education. But she soon found herself swimming in doubts about her career choice.

"What I also learned was that a career in law wasn't for me," Alice said. "It wasn't about arguing the issues and figuring out how to further your cause. It was about finding loopholes and problems with the arguments that were proposed by the other side. It just wasn't my cup of tea."

She decided a conversation with a faculty member at UCLA might ignite a passion for the profession. Instead, she found a new dream, and it took her places she never imagined.

"We started talking about what I was truly interested in," Alice recalled, "and he said, 'Hey, you should walk across the street to the urban planning department, because they study a lot of the things you're interested in—the wealth gap or women's rights or why things happen in a city or why we live in certain places.'"

With that, Alice ditched her plans for law school and discovered a dream worth pursuing—not because there's anything wrong with being a lawyer, but because being a lawyer wasn't *her* dream.

"It was amazing," she said. "My life changed in the course of a forty-five-minute discussion. I went home and reworked my application material that I'd put together for my law school applications and submitted for an urban planning degree and started at UCLA in the fall."

Alice earned her graduate degree, moved to San Francisco "on a whim," and took a temporary job working on a research paper for a company that provided Community Development Financial Institutions (CDFI) funds. That led to an entry-level job as a loan associate and then to a fruitful career combining her passion for affordable housing with her on-the-job training in banking.

Alice eventually spent thirteen years with Citi Community Capital and eleven years as managing director and head of community development banking for JPMorgan Chase. And in 2022, she was named CEO of April Housing, a newly created Blackstone portfolio company committed to the preservation and expansion of affordable housing.

It's safe to say she didn't regret walking away from law school.

For aspiring young leaders, the lesson is obvious: Be willing to pivot toward your true passions. I'll cover that idea in more detail in Principle 8, but the more immediate point is that successful leaders typically live beyond dreams that develop over time, not well-defined dreams that originate at birth or even early in their lives.

That certainly was the case with the leaders interviewed for this book.

Amy Price, for instance, told me she had no definitive plans early in her life—not for college or a career—but she responded to opportunities as they came, embraced challenges and new experiences, and eventually built a career in real estate with BentallGreenOak (BGO), a global real estate investment manager with more than $83 billion of assets under management.

Others had dreams for their careers or their lives that were specific in some ways but broad enough to accommodate the unexpected twists and turns that came their way. And by leaving themselves open to the unexpected, they ended up living beyond their original dreams.

In some ways, they were like great companies.

In *Built to Last*, the classic book on what it takes to build a company with sustained success, authors Jim Collins and Jerry Porras debunk what they call the "great idea" myth. Their research found that having a great idea for a company—a great product or service—is not as important to long-term success as a focus on building a great company.

A great idea without a great company behind it, they say, might bring short-term success, but the company will struggle as market conditions shift. Leaders who focus on building a great company, on the other hand, are nimble enough to tweak their offerings or even pivot in totally new directions, and they are more apt to recruit and empower a pipeline of strong leaders who carry on once the founder is gone.

The same is true for individual leaders. Even more important than having a narrowly defined dream for success is focusing on the principles for building a great life. Whether the dream comes early on, arrives later like a lightning flash, or emerges slowly over time like a jigsaw puzzle, the odds of it becoming a reality depend greatly on how well the leader adheres to some core principles.

I saw this play out in the lives of the leaders I interviewed regardless of their race, gender, country of origin, or socioeconomic background. Consider, for instance, where some of the leaders I interviewed began their journey.

Amy and Alice were raised in the suburbs of Los Angeles, while Leslie Hale and Clarence Otis both grew up in LA's inner city. Gerry Lopez was born in Cuba, and Debra Still in Queens, New York. Diane Batayeh's parents immigrated from Jordan to Detroit; Daryl Carter's parents migrated there from Mississippi.

The twenty-four men and women I interviewed, in fact, had incredibly diverse backgrounds and stories. They had unique struggles and unique privileges. But they also had a great deal in common. They faced many of the same barriers and—more importantly—they built their careers and their lives on similar principles. And while you might face those same barriers, you also can embrace the principles. So no matter what your dreams are or how they change over time, you'll be well prepared to live out and contribute to a better world.

INTERVIEWEES

The ideas and insights in this book are the result of thousands of conversations over the years with hundreds of leaders, not just those I interviewed in 2023 and quoted specifically for this book. I am thankful for them all, but particularly grateful to the twenty-four who consented to the interviews here and were able to coordinate their busy schedules with mine so we could have such rich conversations.

Once I derived the principles I wanted to cover in the book, I had to decide which stories from which leaders to use along the way. Since every leader spoke to almost every principle, I began prioritizing stories for each chapter. I set a goal of ensuring that I used something from everyone I interviewed, while trying to avoid repetition that belabored, rather than reinforced, key points. The challenge was never to find places to use what I learned from these interviews but deciding what to leave out.

The titles and accomplishments of the leaders interviewed are woven into the copy along the way, but I thought it would be helpful to add short bios in one place as a reference. So, with my deep gratitude to each, here are the stars of the book in alphabetical order:

Priscilla Almodovar is the president and CEO of Fannie Mae, the government-sponsored Fortune 50 mortgage company. She grew up in Brooklyn and Long Island, excelled in school, and began her career as an attorney for White & Case, where she rose to partner. She later held high-level roles with the New York State Housing Finance Agency, JPMorgan Chase, and Enterprise Community Partners.

Tom Baltimore is chairman and CEO of Park Hotels & Resorts (NYSE: PK), a REIT that has nearly $9 billion in assets and a portfolio of forty-three premium-branded properties in cities like Orlando, Boston, New York, and Honolulu. He is on the boards for American Express and Comcast and formerly served as lead director of the board of Prudential Financial. He also is the co-founder and former president and CEO of RLJ Lodging Trust. He grew up in the Washington, DC, area, where his father was the pastor of a Baptist church.

Diane Batayeh is CEO of Village Green, which manages apartments, affordable housing, and mixed-use retail space. She grew up in Detroit, where her parents landed after immigrating from Jordan, and started her career with Village Green while she was still in college at the University of Michigan.

Alice Carr is CEO of April Housing, a Blackstone portfolio company that is working to preserve and expand the supply of high-quality affordable housing. Before that, Alice spent thirteen years with Citi Community Capital and eleven years as managing director and head of community development banking for JPMorgan Chase.

Daryl Carter is founder, chairman, and CEO of Avanath Capital Management, one of the leading affordable housing investment firms in the country with more than $4 billion in properties across fourteen states. He grew up in inner-city Detroit and started his professional career with Continental Bank. Later, he co-founded Capri Capital, which he helped grow to $8 billion in diversified real estate equity and eventually was acquired by Centerline Capital Group.

Lili Dunn is president and CEO of Bell Partners, one of the largest apartment companies in the US with approximately eighty-five thousand homes under management. She grew up in the real estate business—her father was a developer and broker in New York. Before joining Bell Partners in 2010, she spent twenty years with AvalonBay Communities (formerly part of Trammell Crow Residential), where she led their transactions, redevelopment, and research functions, among other responsibilities. Lili is the first non-family member in almost fifty years to serve as the CEO of Bell Partners, and with her leadership, the company has completed about $20 billion of transactions and evolved into a global investment management firm.

Tammy Fischer chairs the board of trustees for the National Storage Affiliates Trust (NYSE: NSA) and formerly served as CFO and CEO of the REIT. She began her career at Coopers & Lybrand (now PricewaterhouseCoopers, or PwC) before joining Chateau Communities, one of the largest REITs in the manufactured housing sector. Then, she spent four years as executive vice president and CFO of Vintage Wine Trust.

Leslie Hale is president and CEO of RLJ Lodging Trust and the first African American female CEO of a publicly traded REIT. She grew up in the Compton neighborhood of Los Angeles, then went to college at Howard University, where she's now a member of the board of trustees. She also serves on the board for Delta Airlines. She previously held positions in GE's commercial finance and mergers and acquisitions groups and with Goldman Sachs before joining RLJ in 2005.

Chris Howard is the executive vice president and COO of Arizona State University. He graduated from the Air Force Academy, where he was an Academic All-American, class president, and two-year starter at running back for the football team. In addition to attending Oxford as a Rhodes Scholar, he served eight years on active duty for the air force, including time with the Joint Special Operations Command and as a helicopter pilot. He worked for Bristol Myers Squibb and GE and was president of Hampden-Sydney College and Robert Morris University prior to joining the executive team at ASU.

Lynne Katzmann founded Juniper Communities when she was thirty-two years old. It's the only woman-founded, owned, and led business among the top forty assisted-living companies in the United States. Lynne was inducted into the American Senior Housing Association's Hall of Fame in 2020, and in 2019, she was the first recipient of the McKnight's Women of Distinction Lifetime Achievement Award.

Angela Kleiman became president and CEO of Essex Property Trust (NYSE: ESS), a publicly traded real estate investment trust that primarily invests in apartments on the West Coast. She began her career in real estate in 1992 and worked in a variety of roles, including director for JP Morgan Investment Banking and vice president of JP Morgan Investment Management. She joined Essex in 2009 and served as CFO (2015–2020) and president and COO (2021–2023) before becoming CEO in 2023.

David Kong retired in 2021 after nearly eighteen years as president and CEO of BWH Hotel Group, which has more than four thousand hotels in more than one hundred countries with such brands as Best Western Hotels & Resorts, SureStay Hotels, and WorldHotels. He's now a founder and principal of DEI Advisors, a nonprofit that works to advance the careers of women and other minority groups in the hospitality industry.

Gerry Lopez has served as president of global consumer products for Starbucks, CEO of AMC Entertainment, and CEO of Extended Stay America. He was born in Cuba and grew up in Puerto Rico, and now serves on a variety of corporate boards.

Jodie W. McLean is CEO of EDENS, a real estate firm that started in South Carolina and now has assets across the nation valued at more than $6.5 billion. After joining the firm out of college, she was named president in 2002 and CEO in 2015.

Connie Moore is the former CEO of BRE Properties, a REIT that was based in San Francisco, and now is an active member on several boards in the real estate industry. She started her career with BankAmerica Realty Inc., the predecessor to BRE, before joining Consolidated Capital in 1983. In 1996, while working with Security Capital, she helped with the IPO of the company's East Coast apartment holdings, which became Security Capital Atlantic. She joined BRE as president and COO in 2002, became CEO in 2005, and oversaw the company's 2014 merger with Essex Property Trust (NYSE: ESS).

Clarence Otis grew up in the Watts area of southern Los Angeles and was CEO of Darden Restaurants from 2004 to 2014. Darden, the world's largest full-service restaurant company, includes such brands as Olive Garden, LongHorn Steakhouse, Cheddar's, and The Capital Grille.

Denny Marie Post is the former president and CEO of Red Robin and an advisor and board member to companies and organizations like the Women's Foodservice Forum, Vital Farms, Libbey, and *Travel + Leisure*.

Mary Hogan Preusse retired from REIT investing in 2017 and now spends her time as a strategic advisor to the REIT industry, serving on the boards of Digital Realty, Host Hotels & Resorts, Kimco Realty, and Realty Income and as a senior advisor to Fifth Wall, the venture capital firm. She grew up in the Boston area and began her career as an analyst at Merrill Lynch. She spent ten years on the sell side and later spent seventeen years as the head of Americas Real Estate at APG until her retirement and pivot to board work in 2017.

Amy Price is president of BentallGreenOak (BGO), a global real estate investment company with around $81 billion in assets under management. She previously spent eighteen years with Morgan Stanley, where she was managing director and head of real estate investing for the western United States.

Sumit Roy, who grew up in India, is president and CEO of Realty Income, the largest global net-lease REIT in the S&P 500. He joined Realty Income in 2011 and was named chief investment officer in 2013, president in 2015, and CEO in 2018.

Mit Shah is CEO of Noble Investment Group in Atlanta, which has invested in 170 hotels over the last thirty years and has more than $6 billion in assets under management. Mit is the son of immigrants from India. His father earned a doctorate in the United States and worked as a food scientist before the family took an entrepreneurial turn by buying a motel in Winston-Salem, North Carolina.

Susan Stewart is CEO of SWBC Mortgage in San Antonio and former chair of the Mortgage Bankers Association. She began her career in 1983 as a processor for CitiMortgage but joined SWBC in its infancy in 1989. Under her leadership, it has grown from three employees serving the Texas market to around seven hundred employees in forty-three states with $3 billion in annual mortgage originations.

Debra Still spent nineteen years as president and CEO and now serves as vice chair of Pulte Financial Services, which operates residential mortgage and insurance businesses and has more than a thousand employees throughout the United States. She's also a former chair of the Mortgage Bankers Association and was only the second female in its then one-hundred-year history to serve in that role.

Patricia Will is founder and CEO of Belmont Village Senior Living, which developed and operates more than thirty communities in the United States as well as one in Mexico City. Belmont offers options for assisted living, memory care, personal care, and independent living. She grew up in New York but spent most summers in Mexico, home of her stepfather. (She called this the "bagels and tacos" phase of her life.) Prior to founding Belmont Village, she spent fifteen years as an executive in health-care real estate investments for Houston-based Mischer Development.

BARRIERS "SMARRIERS"

Sumit Roy remembers the phone calls home during his college days, but mainly for their brevity.

"Are you good?" his father would ask.

"Yes, sir," Sumit would say.

"Health is good?"

"Yes, sir."

"Do you need anything?"

"Nope. I'm covered."

"Okay. I'll call you a month from now."

It wasn't that he and his father weren't close (they were) or that their phone conversations never covered more ground (they did). It's just that they usually stuck to the basics because international communication in the late 1980s was so expensive.

As president of San Diego–based Realty Income since 2015 and CEO since 2018, Sumit no longer needs to save his pennies for phone calls to family. Realty Income is an S&P 500 company with more than thirteen thousand commercial properties under long-term net-lease agreements and a market capitalization of $62 billion.

But Sumit didn't start out with the goal of running one of the top real estate investment trusts in the country. When he was earning his undergraduate degree in computer science from Georgia College, a small public liberal arts school, he mainly wanted to stay out of debt. And with the rest of his family in India, communicating with his loved ones was a luxury. They didn't have access to email, and there was no texting and no mobile phones. International phone calls cost more than a dollar per minute, and Sumit's part-time job on campus only paid minimum wage—$3.35 an hour with a maximum of twenty hours a week.

Sumit's father was educated in the United States, but he returned to India to work for a company that manufactured cranes. He married and started a family that grew to include Sumit and his three sisters. India, however, was a closed economy when Sumit was growing up, and financial resources were tight in their middle-class family.

Sumit, who excelled in math and physics, wanted to go to the United States for his postsecondary education, but he and his parents had to figure out how they would pay for it. While Georgia College awarded him a scholarship that covered his tuition, he still had to pay for his housing, books, meals, and the occasional phone call home.

"The biggest issue for us as a family was obviously affordability," Sumit told me. "It was very important to get the academic scholarship so that the burden on my family was going to be as minimal as possible."

Sumit was determined not to allow his dream to become a financial burden on his family. He never asked for financial help, and when his father sent money, Sumit put it in a certificate of deposit in the bank so it would earn interest until he could give it back.

"I felt confident enough in telling my dad, 'I've got it,'" Sumit told me. "I didn't know how it was going to happen, but I knew I was going to figure it out, whatever it took. I washed dishes in the cafeteria. I worked in the bookstore loading books. I picked watermelon in the midst of summer. And I can tell you in Georgia, it gets really, really hot, and you get seven dollars per hour for picking watermelons. That's backbreaking, but I did what I needed to do to make ends meet."

What you might have noticed in Sumit's story is that he never describes his family's lack of financial resources as a barrier in his journey. And that mindset was one of the most common themes I found in my interviews with successful leaders. They didn't sugarcoat the path to their success, but they didn't dwell on the things that stood in their way.

Lili Dunn, now president and CEO of Bell Partners, summed up what several of the leaders told me: "I don't dwell on past barriers and challenges. I look at the opportunities ahead, stay positive, and find a way to make a difference. With hard work, creativity, and persistence, anything is possible."

And in what "space" do these leaders live?

Think of it as a "no excuses" zone.

Here's how Daryl Carter, founder and CEO of Avanath Capital Management, describes that zone: "I guess I've always had a focus of not looking at the barriers," he said, "but focusing on the solutions, because in real life, everybody has barriers."

Connie Moore, the former CEO of BRE Properties and now an active member on several boards in the real estate industry, also said she never gave much thought to barriers.

"For me, I've never considered anything that's occurred in my life as a barrier," she told me. "They were hurdles. I didn't really learn to jump them. But I did go around them, right?"

Sumit also went around them. After graduating from Georgia College, he earned a master's degree from the University of Georgia and started his career as a technology consultant. Later, he earned an MBA from the University of Chicago, where he began to learn about investment banking. That led him to roles with Merrill Lynch and UBS Investment Bank before joining Realty Income.

He faced a few barriers along the way—the stress of waiting on his green card and getting laid off by Merrill Lynch in 2003—but like Lili, Connie, Daryl, and the others I interviewed, Sumit doesn't dwell much on the obstacles.

Nevertheless, the barriers faced by aspiring leaders are very real and worth acknowledging, not so you can use them as a crutch or a target for blame when things don't go as planned, but because they are reality.

In fact, my research found that all leaders typically encounter barriers that fit in six categories—economic, sociological, psychological, cultural, bias-based, and market-based—and those barriers can be particularly difficult for women and minorities.

The leaders I interviewed don't spend much time thinking much about those barriers, but it was clear they didn't ignore them when they faced them in life. It seemed they intuitively knew they were there, and they recognized them for what they were. They kept them in the proper perspective as they focused on solutions to get past the barriers. And they made the most of the lessons that emerged from overcoming them.

Directly or indirectly, every leader interviewed described experiencing barriers that fell within at least two of the categories. And their stories helped me identify the principles and skills that are key to living beyond your dreams regardless of the challenges you might face in your unique journey.

So while this book won't dwell on the barriers, it's worth taking a quick look at the six categories before moving on to the principles and skills that emerged from the lives of the leaders.

> **Economic Barriers**—Money matters. It's not the most important thing, but as George Bailey noted in *It's a Wonderful Life*, money "comes in pretty handy down here, bub!"
>
> Scholarships and grants, for instance, might cover some educational costs, but financial concerns still can add pressure to an already stress-filled academic life. When it's time to invest in opportunities, access to capital often determines if and how

quickly leaders move forward. And when leaders hit setbacks, financial resources play a role in if or how quickly they rebound and relaunch.

Twelve of the interviewees spoke of economic barriers, primarily in the context of their family's situation growing up. It was common for them to talk about what they learned from parents about the value of money, hard work, gratitude, and giving back.

Sociological Barriers—Leaders born into low-income families face obvious financial barriers, but they also encounter other obstacles related to the social structures around them.

For instance, they are less likely to attend the top schools or be surrounded by other students with self-discipline, good grades, and good behavior. They are more likely to be exposed to friends and relatives who are in gangs, who use drugs, and who have untreated mental health issues. And they are more likely to experience abuse, neglect, or trauma as a child that impacts their mental and emotional well-being.

Fourteen of the interviewees spoke of sociological barriers, but none talked about abuse, neglect, or trauma—not even the one who was raised by relatives from the time she was a baby because her mother left the family. In fact, those in my interview pool typically had the advantage of a strong family network of support, although in a couple of cases the family prioritized joining the workforce over pursuing higher education or starting a company. And a few of the women had parents who thought their daughters should marry rather than go to college and work outside the home. But none of those had parents who actively opposed their choices.

Some, however, talked about the negative impact their parents' divorces had on their journeys, the lack of exposure they had growing up in inner cities, and the hierarchies (dare I say snobbery) in certain social circles of higher education.

Psychological Barriers—Pressure is a powerful force, and psychological pressure can hit leaders from many different directions.

Many women, for instance, struggle with the pressure of competing demands between their work and family lives. Some leaders feel the pressure to succeed, perhaps because they come from a family filled with successful leaders or perhaps because they represent their family's first real professional success story. And for some there's a concern that failure won't be followed by a second chance.

David Kong, who spent nearly eighteen years as president and CEO of BWH Hotel Group, echoed what others described about psychological barriers when he said, "I think the most significant barriers that I encountered were the ones that were self-imposed."

Psychological barriers were the second most commonly mentioned among the interviewees, with sixteen of the twenty-four sharing stories that fit in this category. Most of these revolved around issues of self-confidence, like a fear of speaking in public, a fear of failure, or feeling like they weren't worthy (imposter syndrome).

It's worth noting that there's some overlap with all the barriers, but I found the most when it came to psychological, sociological, and cultural. For instance, divorced parents created barriers that might be considered sociological, but that also created psychological constraints. And parents who pushed marriage and family over education and careers for their daughters could be considered cultural or sociological barriers along with psychological challenges.

Cultural Barriers—In an increasingly global society, aspiring leaders study with, socialize with, and work with and for other leaders who have different styles of communicating, different values, different faith backgrounds, and different traditions.

This could be as obvious as a Pakistani computer engineer working in rural Iowa, but there are many other examples. A woman raised on a farm will encounter cultural barriers when she moves to New York City, just as someone who grew up in an inner city will experience barriers when working alongside suburbanites.

Only nine of the interviewees mentioned barriers that fit in this category. Most were immigrants or children of immigrants. Two-time CEO Gerry Lopez, for instance, was raised by Cuban parents who immigrated to Miami before settling in Puerto Rico. In school, he read from textbooks written in English, but the oral instruction was always in Spanish. Thus, he learned to read the

English language at a high level long before he became proficient in speaking it.

Some of the cultural barriers provided examples of how leaders view challenges differently than others might suspect. For instance, Sumit, who was born in Calcutta (now Kolkata), had only flown once and had never been outside of India when he traveled halfway around the world by himself to a rural southern college town that was the capital of Georgia during the American Civil War.

"I will tell you, it was very different," he told me. "It was very new."

Different and new no doubt created a few barriers in his journey, but he mentioned nothing but positive memories about his time in Georgia.

"I've obviously led a very blessed life, because the people took to me and they helped me along," Sumit told me. "I was always invited to Thanksgiving dinners in this small town called Milledgeville, seventy miles south of Atlanta, and the people I worked with always looked out for me and made sure that I had my twenty hours so I could make my living."

Bias Barriers—Conscious or unconscious bias based on race, ethnicity, gender, sexual orientation, or ability can limit opportunities such as mentorships, sponsorships, stretch assignments, and promotions. Over time, the cumulative effect also can hinder the self-esteem and confidence needed to take risks or persist through trials. Even the perception of bias can create mental hurdles.

In Steve White's introduction to his book *Uncompromising*, the former CEO of Comcast West wrote about the cumulative effect of bias on his leadership. Like the leaders I interviewed, he didn't dwell on it, but he acknowledged it was a factor that shaped his journey.

"It's what some would label as the 'burden of my Black experience,'" White wrote. "And the only way I know how to sum it up is with that one word: *exhaustion*."[1]

Given the backgrounds of the leaders interviewed, it's not surprising this category came up the most—nineteen of the twenty-four shared examples. Not all of the examples had to do with race or gender, however. In some cases, for instance, the bias was against a perceived lack of certain skills or experiences.

Furthermore, while the examples of overt bias were all too numerous, it's also interesting that some leaders spoke of their own biases as barriers to their success. And in a positive context, they talked of co-workers and bosses who stood up for them and about their refusal to be defined by the traits others, in their ignorance, held against them. As Fannie Mae CEO Priscilla Almodovar put it, "I've never let being a woman define me."

Market Barriers—Some of the barriers on the path to a leader's ascent have little to do with who they are, where they come from, or who they work

---

1 Steve White, *Uncompromising: How an Unwavering Commitment to Your Why Leads to an Impactful Life and a Lasting Legacy* (Nashville: Post Hill Press, 2022).

with and more to do with larger winds that blow the economic sands around them.

Only twelve leaders mentioned examples that fit into this category, which was interesting since they all were high-level leaders during a global pandemic, most managed teams through at least one economic recession, and some were laid off by an employer experiencing tough times. In other words, whether they mentioned such barriers or not, they all faced unfavorable market conditions.

For instance, Sumit was newly married, his wife was going back to school for her master's degree, and he had started a job with Merrill Lynch just two days before the 9/11 attacks in 2001. He survived that uncertainty, but two years later, in January 2003, he was let go during another round of layoffs.

"That's when you feel like your back's against the wall," Sumit told me.

But like the other leaders interviewed, he didn't dwell on the barrier for very long.

"You have a loan to pay and you don't have income coming in, and it really does create this strength," he said. "A lot of it was my family—my new wife. That's where you draw a lot of your strength. But the one thing that I always was able to lean on was my academic background. The experiences that academia had afforded me was, again, something that nobody could take away from me."

It's that type of attitude that resonated throughout the interviews and that I describe in more detail

in several chapters, particularly the one on dealing
with the hand you are dealt.

The barriers are very real, but living out the principles
described by these leaders, as you will see, provides a path over
or around them until before you know it, they hardly even
matter because you find yourself somewhere beyond what you
ever dreamed.

Part II

Part II

CHARACTER COUNTS

It's common for leadership books to stress the importance of character—our disposition to think, feel, and act in morally and ethically acceptable ways.[1] But we can't buy character from a store like a block of cheese or a fine bottle of wine. It's something we develop over time, and we build it by drawing from a variety of sources and experiences.

For instance, Lynne Katzmann, founder and CEO of Juniper Communities, can trace her sense of moral obligation about work to a number of experiences in her background—books she read, lessons she learned in college and graduate school, advice people shared with her, and things she did early in her career.

The most interesting, however, has to do with what she observed, and it is perhaps best exemplified by something her parents never actually told her when she was growing up.

Lynne's parents were immigrants, coming to the United States in the late 1930s along with her grandparents from Germany. But her mother was five when she immigrated, and her father was nine when he arrived in the US. So while her grandparents spoke German in the home, her mother and father always spoke English—flawless English—and they

---

1   Taya R. Cohen and Lily Morse, "Moral Character: What It Is and What It Does," Carnegie Mellon University, July 12, 2014, https://doi.org/10.1184/ R1/6706985.v1.

never told her they weren't born in America or that they had escaped the horrors of the Holocaust as children.

"They just thought I knew," she told me. "It was osmosis. But I didn't know that as a child. So it didn't inform me in terms of their story; it informed me in terms of their actions and the attitudes and values they instilled in me, which I think have had a huge impact on who I am today."

Lynne's family gave her plenty of advice about life, but nothing more powerful than the "actions and attitudes and values" that shaped her character.

Indeed, while qualities like intelligence, business acumen, and social skills were important to Lynne and all the leaders interviewed for this book, the moral underpinnings—things like integrity, ethics, honesty, humility, gratitude, and responsibility—emerged from their stories as a foundational key to success.

David Kong, the former president and CEO of Best Western Hotels, put it this way: "If you want to be successful, first and foremost you have to have the right character. You have to be honest. You have to have integrity. You have to prove that you can be trusted."

Regardless of their job titles, their roles, the organizations with which they are associated, or the industries they find themselves in, the success of leaders is more often traced to who they "are" rather than what they "do." Who they are—their character—shapes everything they do and how they do it.

Lynne's character clearly shaped her actions and attitudes when building Juniper Communities, one of the most impactful senior-care companies in the world. A sense of purpose that came at least in part from her parents and grandparents—the belief that doing the right thing involves serving the common good—informed every aspect of her entrepreneurial journey.

"Making the world a better place has always been a fundamental part of what's driven me," she said.

Six years before entrepreneur and author John Elkington coined the phrase "triple bottom line"[2] in 1994, Lynne was a thirty-two-year-old idealist launching a company around the belief in "doing well by doing good." Juniper Communities, which now operates twenty-seven senior communities in four states, has innovated and evolved with the times, but it has always held true to Lynne's dual purpose.

"We have a responsibility on more than one front," she told me. "It's not just about revenue and profitability. So that sense of doing well by doing good has been what has propelled me and Juniper. That's the core value that drives our company. We need to make money—we're a for-profit company, and we've done very well financially—but we have to do it in a way that serves a greater good."

Lynne's belief that a business can make a profit and do good was rooted in her upbringing but nurtured and supported by several other "actions and attitudes and values" she witnessed while growing up, most notably an entrepreneurial spirit that runs deep in her heritage.

Fred Katzmann, Lynne's father, was an entrepreneur and inventor who worked for Fairchild Semiconductors, Monsanto, and Singer before owning Ballantine Labs. He had many patents and was part of an international cadre of people moving the digital world forward from the 1950s onward. Lynne traveled with him as a preteen while he helped set up Monsanto's electrical engineering division in cities around the world.

Meanwhile, her maternal grandmother, Oma Gustel, founded a business in the 1920s with her two sisters. Oma worked her entire life, rode a motorcycle into her seventies, and is celebrated throughout Juniper Communities each April

---

2   John Elkington, "25 Years Ago I Coined the Phrase 'Triple Bottom Line.' Here's Why It's Time to Rethink It," *Harvard Business Review*, June 25, 2018, https://hbr.org/2018/06/25-years-ago-i-coined-the-phrase-triple-bottom-line-heres-why-im-giving-up-on-it.

on her birthday. But she was also "very much a wife, mother, and member of the community," Lynne said, and a role model in those areas for her granddaughter as well. Thus, Lynne never doubted that she could build a career and raise a family, she told me, even if she "didn't know how to accomplish it."

She figured that out just fine, of course, and she did it while raising her son Andrew as a single mother. And, by the way, when Lynne was inducted into the American Senior Housing Association's Hall of Fame, she was introduced at the ceremony by her son, who now is a vice president with Columbia Pacific Advisors, a Seattle-based investment firm.

All the traits that became definable aspects of Lynne's character—and that's a long list that goes well beyond her moral obligation to "do good" through her work—set her up for success in life, but she didn't set out to create that success by building a business in the senior living sector. That came later as her education, experiences, and interests began weaving their way together with her fundamental beliefs.

Early on, it looked like Lynne might build a career in the government or nonprofit worlds by crafting economic policies around health care for developing nations. She was a good student growing up, and her family emphasized the importance of intellectual pursuits and independence of thought. So she took her idealistic bent to Tufts University, where she earned two degrees in just three years, and then to the London School of Economics, where she worked on a master's degree in social policy planning in developing countries.

That led to an opportunity to pursue a PhD in health policy while working with Brian Abel-Smith, the British economist and one of the twentieth century's most influential advocates for social welfare. She researched her dissertation on the economics of health care while living in Germany, Norway, and England, then came back to the United States with no definitive plan for what she would do next.

Lynne was at a dinner party in Oregon when she met a young geologist whose grandfather had a controlling interest in a public health-care company. He had agreed to oversee the company for his grandfather, but he had no background in health care. Lynne was still in her mid-twenties, but she agreed to move to New York and help run the company. And she spent the next few years working with the family and its businesses, including two years of working on venture investment projects.

"I've been very lucky," she told me. "It's been a series of strange coincidences or opportunities that I didn't plan, for the most part, but of which I was able to take advantage."

In 1988, after the family's business sold, she raised $440,000 from investors and started Juniper based on the belief that "aging is not a disease in search of a cure" but a normal stage of life "in search of respect." In the late 1980s, however, there weren't many options for assisted living. Seniors could move to retirement communities (mostly in Florida) or nursing homes. Lynne believed there was a "better way of doing it."

Juniper started by purchasing undermanaged buildings where seniors lived and leased them to local or regional companies that ran them in a more sustainable and profitable fashion. Those projects were successful, and she continued to raise money by seeking investors who saw the social significance of her dream of promoting better living options for seniors.

"They invested in me because I was a woman, because I was socially responsible, because I had a mission, and I think I had a pretty good business plan," she said.

When Lynne talks about Juniper, it's impossible to ignore the harmony she's found in building a successful business while striving for a higher purpose.

For instance, on the one hand she talks in great detail about the complexities of the senior living industry: building management, regulatory issues, technology issues, the importance of data-driven insights, the need to understand health systems, and the variety of payment sources. And she talks effortlessly about financial results, revenue streams, and cash flow that services debt.

Sounds like quintessential business topics, right?

On the other hand, all of that comes in the context of an overriding premise of improving the quality of life for seniors.

"Essentially, the American system is running out of money and we focus on intervention, not prevention," she said. "The way to save money and the way to provide a better life for people is to focus on the other side, on the things that keep people healthy rather than the things that treat them when they're sick."

Thus, Juniper has communities that offer chronic-care planning, management, and monitoring to help seniors manage their lifestyle. Its Connect4Life program has cut hospitalizations by 50 percent and readmissions by 80 percent, which, she points out, would save the economy between $10 billion and $15 billion a year if spread across the American population.

"My belief is that together we can make the world a better place," she told me. "We won't change everything, but we will create an environment that is better for people to live in, that is financially fair, and that provides returns to our funding sources who are equally invested in what we do as much as our residents and our team members."

LOOKING FOR CHARACTER ALIGNMENT

While Lynne's character shaped the type of business she founded and how she runs it, Tammy Fischer's values played a key role in why she chose to work with a company that already existed.

Tammy, the CEO of National Storage Affiliates, was a real estate auditor for Coopers & Lybrand (now

PricewaterhouseCoopers, or PwC) in the late 1980s when her first husband died in an accident shortly after their daughter was born. She already had been thinking about cutting back on her work hours and was looking at a role with Chateau Communities, but now she had to factor in how she would raise her daughter as a single mother.

Chateau, which at the time was one of the largest real estate investment trusts specializing in manufactured home communities, had been one of her clients, so she knew the management team and saw the company as perfectly aligned with her values.

"I really picked Chateau as the place where I wanted to work because they were really nice people and integrity was a big part of what they did," she told me. "They didn't do it because they had to. They did it because it was how they lived their lives. Those were their values."

Tammy became Chateau's executive vice president and chief financial officer in 1993, and she played a key role in taking the company public. When Chateau sold in 2003, she took the CFO role for Vintage Wine Trust and then transitioned to National Storage Affiliates (NSA), first as CFO, and in 2020, she was named CEO and chair of the company's board. With each move, Tammy found herself attracted to hardworking, high-integrity organizations that matched the character traits she stressed in her own life.

Like Lynne Katzmann, those traits took root early in Tammy's life, partly from the influences of her family and partly from friends.

Traits like resilience and hard work—what she sometimes refers to as her "scrappy nature"—originated with her family experiences, although that family took a nontraditional form.

Tammy was the youngest of five siblings living in an apartment in Tennessee when her mother left the family. Her father didn't think he could raise the children, so the older siblings went to live with their grandfather, a coal miner in Ohio, and

Tammy, who was less than a year old, ended up in Michigan with her aunt and uncle and their two sons.

"They were good to me and always treated me like I was their own child," she told me. "I was their only girl. My uncle's parents and his sister lived nearby. They just took me in and never, never missed a beat to be honest with you."

By the time she was in junior high it was clear that Tammy was a strong student, but her family had no history with higher education and didn't see it as a priority.

"Their attitude was the minute you're done with high school, you start working," she said. "You get a job. But I became friends with kids who had different aspirations. They were teeing themselves up to go to college, and I was like, 'Hmm! That's an interesting thought process.' So I kind of latched on to that group, and it changed the way I thought about education and how hard I wanted to work at it. My peers and the teachers in high school were amazing. They had high standards. They expected you to do your best. And they encouraged and supported me to get a higher education."

Now, when Tammy advises the next generation of leaders, she often stresses those same character traits.

"I have a conversation about staying true to your values," she said. "And for me, it's what we weave through the culture at NSA—our stated values of accountability, integrity, humility, and compassion. I just wouldn't sacrifice that to accomplish other things."

THE HOW MATTERS

One reason character provides a foundation for the success of a leader's journey is that it becomes the basis for how you deal with barriers and challenges along the way.

If you lack integrity as a bedrock value, for instance, you are more likely to cut corners to solve problems rather than draw an ethical line in the sand. And if you demonstrate a lack of integrity, you can't build trust with the people who work with or for you. That's why Lili Dunn calls integrity the "price of admission" to work at Bell Partners, where she is president and CEO.

"There are many times when you are faced with choices that no one may know about," she told me. "You have to always look in the mirror, knowing you never compromised your integrity."

The challenge, of course, is maintaining your values when others around you are not, especially when standing your ground might create new barriers while giving in might temporarily smooth your path. When that happens, leaders like Lili have found that it's not only important to do the right thing but to figure out the right way to do the right thing.

When Lili began her career in real estate, very few women held high-level positions, especially in investments and finance. And like many professional women of that era, she often faced challenges related to inclusion, authority, and inappropriate behavior.

"I had to learn how to fit in yet stand up and be myself, never forgetting the responsibility to help others in similar situations," she told me.

When she was in her twenties, she was often excluded from social and business outings with her male counterparts.

"I felt a responsibility to say something," she said. "It was an awkward situation because if you were seen as too aggressive, the situation became even worse. The 'how' really mattered—I needed to be heard in a way that would be taken seriously yet not make it uncomfortable for all involved."

Lili has navigated many situations requiring poise and tact. She recounted a story about one of her business meetings at AvalonBay, a REIT that specialized in apartment communities. At twenty-seven years old, Lili had already become a vice president—an unusual accomplishment for a young woman at the time. She was hosting a business meeting and, she said, "a large group of older men walked into the room and they all started handing me their coats and asked me to get them some coffee while they waited for Mr. Dunn. I took their coats, smiled, and politely explained that the meeting was with Ms. Dunn, me."

She said she would be happy to get their coffee if someone would run down the street and grab some bagels for the group. Everyone laughed, and the men learned a valuable lesson about not making assumptions.

"You can't demand respect; you need to earn it," Lili says. "However, you do need to stand up for yourself while remembering that the 'how' really matters."

Several of the women I interviewed, including Lili, spoke of times when men made inappropriate sexual advances, something that's no longer seen as acceptable in the workplace but that still happens all too often.

Lynne Katzmann, for instance, lost a scholarship while working on her doctorate degree, she said, "when the head of the Free University of Berlin hit on me and I told him no." Lynne simply found another scholarship and went back to work.

Connie Moore, meanwhile, spent nearly ten years as CEO of BRE Properties, a REIT based in San Francisco, and has more than forty years of experience in the real estate industry. She still recalls the first time she felt an unwanted hand on her knee while sitting at a table with two of her bosses.

"I just shifted and made it pretty clear, *thank you, but no thank you*," she told me. "I knew I couldn't insult these guys. I had to work with them. I could get pissed, but I had to work with them every single day. I eased into basically saying no without hurting anybody's feelings so I could keep working, because for me it was about the job. I had a goal."

While the job and goals are important, they aren't more important than your character. But Connie believes you can stand up for yourself without wearing your feelings on your sleeve in ways that make situations even worse.

"Life is not fair," Connie said. "But you can overcome it. And you get to decide if you are really willing to put up with something or if you have the self-confidence to make a change and to do something different. But if you know you're doing the right thing it will pan out in the end. It just will."

DREAM CATCHERS

Indigenous people like the Anishinaabe in the Great Lakes region were probably the first to make hoops of willow and weave a spiderweb-like net in the center. They decorated these hoops with sacred items like feathers to create protective charms for their sleeping infants, and tradition holds that these dream catchers blocked negative dreams while allowing only the good ones in.

In honor of that tradition, I'll end the next eleven chapters with a summary of what stood out the most to me—the nuggets about each principle that my personal beyond-your-dreams dream catcher allowed to pass through. What stood out to you, of course, might be different, so feel free to add to the list. I'll also include a few questions for you to consider before moving to the next chapter.

> Who you are shapes everything you do and how you do it. Moral underpinnings like integrity, ethics, honesty, humility, gratitude, and responsibility are foundational success.

> Your character is formed in part by the actions, attitudes, and values you absorb from the people you respect most; likewise, your actions, attitudes, and values influence the character of others.

> When making choices about career options, prioritize value-alignment.

▷ The values you prioritize are the values you will live out.

▷ Integrity is essential to building trust and therefore the "price of admission" for working with any worthy organization.

▷ Your values will be put to the test. Learn to stand up for them but in appropriate and respectful ways.

QUESTIONS

1. What actions, attitudes, and values were instilled in you that most greatly shaped your character?
2. Do your values align with the values of your employers?
3. How are your values regularly challenged at work, and how can you make appropriate and respectful stands for what you believe?
4. Who do you trust to help you navigate such challenges?

PRINCIPLE 2

ASK *WHY NOT?*

David Kong stood for hours because that's what the job required. Busing tables and washing dishes at a restaurant in Honolulu, however, left plenty of room for daydreaming, so David took it upon himself to give direction to all the ideas drifting through his teenage mind while he performed what were mostly repetitive tasks.

David had come to Hawaii from Hong Kong, where he was born and raised after his parents fled from Communist China in the 1940s. David's father managed a shop, often working seven days a week, and his mother taught school during the day and then tutored students who needed extra attention. They worked hard, showered their four sons with unconditional love, and saved their money with a simple but powerful goal in mind: send their boys abroad for college so they could have a better life.

Thus, David arrived in Hawaii in 1970 with his family's work ethic, the intellectual curiosity and faith that resulted from his Jesuit high school education, and a deep appreciation for his parents and the sacrifices they had made. But he had no friends, no connections, no return ticket, and very little money.

"It was pretty scary," David told me.

When he was growing up in Hong Kong, David's close-knit family often went to lunch on Sundays at one of the nicer

57

hotel restaurants, and those outings sparked his interest in the hospitality industry. A friend of his father's had worked for hotels in Hawaii, and at his suggestion, David took off for the islands. He enrolled at the University of Hawaii, found a job at the Hilton Hawaiian Village, and began asking the question that inevitably hits us all on the journey from youth to adulthood: *What's next?*

The answer, he discovered, was found in another question: *Why not?*

When others might have seen closed doors, long odds, insurmountable barriers, or unreachable goals, David saw opportunities by framing his choices with the rhetorical question.

"I have always asked myself, 'why not?'" David told me. "So I would look at the restaurant manager and say, 'why not?' And I became the restaurant manager."

David didn't stop with the question, of course, but regularly asking it proved pivotal in a career that included more than seventeen years as president and CEO of BWH Hotel Group, the parent organization for Best Western Hotels & Resorts and more than a dozen other hotel brands. His *why not* attitude led him to take the measured risks that defined his career and shaped many of the decisions he made as a leader.

What makes the question so significant, however, is that asking it often shook him free of a self-imposed barrier to his success: a lack of self-confidence.

"Sometimes you sell yourself short," David told me. "I learned how to shift my thinking. I learned how to overcome my imposter syndrome."

David joined the hotel industry in Hawaii at a time when Asians often were seen as hardworking, knowledgeable, and dependable but lacking in other qualities required of high-level leadership. Big hotels were opening on the islands at the time, but people of European descent ended up in most of the key positions.

David saw no future for himself in Hawaii, so he took a good job as the food and beverage director at the Dunfey Dallas Hotel, which would become an Omni Hotel. Two years later, the company offered him a promotion to become resident manager at a property in San Francisco. His wife, meanwhile, worked at a Hyatt at the time. When he told her about the opportunity in California, she mentioned that the assistant food and beverage director had just left the Hyatt Regency Dallas. Maybe he should apply for that, she said.

On the surface, the job in San Francisco was much better. The role with Hyatt would take him two steps down the ladder and result in a 35 percent cut in pay. On the other hand, he considered Hyatt an industry innovator with better pathways to executive leadership.

Why not take a step back if it can lead somewhere better?

He took that job and spent the next nineteen years rising through the managerial and executive ranks of Hyatt.

"I just had to figure out what to do and be constructive," he told me. "I had to take charge of my life. So I didn't let that bother me too much. I couldn't change people's biases about wanting to have a white person in a position. I could not change it in any way. So if I wanted to make this my career, I had to do something about it. If I couldn't make it in Hawaii, I could make it somewhere else. That gave me the motivation to move to Dallas. And as it turned out, that was actually wonderful for my career."

Hyatt offered more exposure and more opportunities, and he took full advantage of them. When they needed someone to reengineer the company's business process, for instance, David said *why not?* and took on the challenge.

"I left the comfort of a role as a live-in general manager, where I could take the elevator to work and order room service for dinner, and went to work for the corporate office, taking a job that nobody knew how to do because it was a brand-new thing," he said.

When he was asked to build the database capabilities to improve Hyatt's sales and marketing and later when he was asked to launch Hyatt's first website, he again said *why not?* and stepped into what at the time was groundbreaking territory.

David was an associate vice president in 2000 when it became clear he had reached his ceiling with Hyatt, so he spent a year as a consultant with KPMG and then joined the team at Best Western as vice president for strategic services. After five promotions in less than four years, he was named president and CEO of Best Western International when the role opened in 2004.

Under his leadership, BWH Hotel Group grew from one brand to eighteen, with around 4,500 hotels in more than a hundred countries. They regularly set company records for financial performance and guest satisfaction ratings, and David became an industry leader in advocating for diversity and inclusion.

Still, there were times along the way when he lacked self-confidence as a leader because his personality didn't fit the traditional mold. Hyatt brought in outgoing, dynamic, charismatic leaders, for instance, while David said his Asian heritage had taught him to be reserved. He also realized he hadn't learned to build a network of supporters while at Hyatt.

When he went to Best Western, David worked more intentionally at finding sponsors and advocates, but he recognized it would be a mistake to fundamentally change his leadership style.

His response? *Why not lead with my God-given personality?*

Buying into that belief and living it out, however, took time.

"I was on CEO panels many, many times at many industry conferences, and all around me were white men," he said. "So I stuck out like a sore thumb. I used to be very conscious of that, and I felt like, 'Oh, I'm an imposter up here.' But I learned to embrace my unique self. I learned that if I look different, then let me bring a different perspective to the table."

Soon, his differences became competitive advantages when building and leading teams that executed at high levels.

"It doesn't take a charismatic person to be a leader," he said. "I found you could be a quiet, thoughtful leader who is patient and has humility. Over time, I think people appreciate that more."

At the same time, David said, you have to bring "substance to the table." You have to achieve results, and not just any results, he said, but "breakthrough" results.

"So the ability to formulate strategies and persuade others to come on board," he said, "all those things are also really important."

Asking *why not?* helped David find the courage to take risks and reinvent himself daily so that he could consistently bring fresh ideas and strategies to his work, while staying true to himself along the way. This approach to leadership, he said, fit perfectly with a couple of lessons he adapted from Amazon founder Jeff Bezos.

In a letter to shareholders in 2016, for instance, Bezos famously addressed the battle against complacency faced by all leaders (and companies).

"Day 2 is stasis," Bezos wrote. "Followed by irrelevance. Followed by excruciating, painful decline. Followed by death. And that is why it is always Day 1."[1]

David believes in treating every day as Day 1.

"On Day 1, you are so excited about going to work, because everything is possible," he said. "You have to be scrappy and you have to work harder, but you are excited about that day because it's Day 1. So how do you sustain that? Well, I believe that you have to constantly reinvent yourself to achieve Day 1. Whether it's a company or an individual, you have to give

---

1   "2016 Letter to Stakeholders," Amazon, April 17, 2017, https://www. aboutamazon.com/news/company-news/2016-letter-to-shareholders.

yourself that newfound enthusiasm by trying something new, something really meaningful."

That requires a willingness to be misunderstood, which is another maxim from Bezos that has David's full endorsement.

"It means leaders should have bold ideas," he told me. "But bold ideas take time to take hold, and sometimes they're misunderstood. You have to give it time, and eventually you prove yourself right. And that is certainly true in my case."

In other words, when everyone else says, "Why should we do that?" you need to focus on the possibilities, stick to what you believe, and say, "Why not?"

WHY NOT BE UNCOMFORTABLE?

David learned how to be comfortable being uncomfortable, and that's not unusual among successful leaders—or their parents. Indeed, like most of these principles, it's often something the leaders learned from their parents.

David's parents taught him the value of sacrificing for a bigger goal when they invested their lives into providing him and his brothers with the opportunity to go to college. Several other leaders shared stories of how their parents intentionally sacrificed so that their children might have more.

It's the American Dream, right?

Mit Shah, the CEO of Noble Investment Group in Atlanta, learned about sacrifice from his parents and extended family members. His grandparents, for instance, sacrificed when they borrowed money from friends and family to buy a plane ticket so Bharat Shah, Mit's father, could leave their rural manufacturing town in India in 1964 to attend college in the United States.

Mit's father, who adapted to the cultural differences and earned a master's degree from the University of Tennessee and a doctorate from Utah State, could have been satisfied with the comforts of a career as a food scientist. By 1979, Bharat

Shah was earning a modest salary of about $28,000 a year, and the family lived in a $50,000 ranch-style home in North Carolina. They weren't wealthy, but ten-year-old Mit had a bicycle to ride through the neighborhood and considered himself the happiest kid on the planet.

That's when his dad quit his job and his parents borrowed money from friends and family to become the proud owners of the Winkler Motor Inn in Winston-Salem, North Carolina.

Mit grew up working for his parents at the motel. He manned the front desk on the weekends, washed sheets, cleaned rooms, and did whatever else was needed to be part of a "living, breathing family business that was open 365 days a year, twenty-four hours a day."

Uncomfortable? Sure. But Mit calls it "a beautiful American Dream story."

Furthermore, it was the perfect training ground for his career, especially when it came to his willingness to personally take risks and be uncomfortable.

"Taking on risk and having ownership is something you either choose to do or not to do," Mit told me. "I saw the good, the bad, and sometimes the ugly in that, but it reinforced to me that taking risks with yourself and hard work and believing in yourself can really have extraordinary outcomes."

When Mit left home for college, his parents encouraged him to pursue a career in medicine, but he quickly realized that wasn't a good fit for his skills and passions. Instead, he pivoted while at Wake Forest University and earned a degree in economics. He entered a tight job market in 1991, but a small investment firm in Atlanta was looking for someone with some very specific attributes: a business or economics degree and five to eight years of experience in hotel operations.

"This was really just serendipity," Mit said.

If so, it was a serendipity born of his parents' willingness to ask, *Why not buy a hotel and pursue the American Dream?* Regardless, the opportunity fed Mit's entrepreneurial spirit.

He thrived and soon found himself taking risks in pursuit of his own dreams.

About two years into his professional career, Mit brought the firm his analysis for a deal to build a hotel as part of a new community near Atlanta. The leadership team felt they were over-allocated in the area and turned down the opportunity, but Mit believed it was too good to pass up. He went to the company's founder to make his case, and the founder agreed it was a good project. Then he made an offer Mit wasn't expecting: What if we back you to do it on your own?

It was Mit Shah's *why not* moment.

He invested personal savings, borrowed money from his parents, and, with the firm's backing, he created Noble Investment Group and broke ground on the Hampton Inn Peachtree City. The contractor went bankrupt in the middle of the project, but it opened a year later, in July 1994, and never had less than 90 percent occupancy.

Mit repaid his parents for their investment, and one Hampton Inn led to another. Noble Investment Group has invested in approximately two hundred hotels over the last thirty years and has more than $6 billion in assets. And Mit built a career and a company on the foundation of a belief that ran at least three generations deep in his family: It's okay to be uncomfortable.

WHY NOT SPEAK AGAINST YOUR FEARS?

The reluctance to embrace discomfort—or to be misunderstood, as David Kong put it—typically is tied to fears that are self-imposed.

Mary Hogan Preusse, for instance, began her career with a fear of public speaking. In fact, even though she's the founder of Sturgis Partners and now sits on boards for such well-regarded REITs as Host Hotels, Digital Realty, Kimco Realty, and Realty Income, she didn't feel like she conquered that fear until around 2021.

Mary traced her fear of speaking to her preschool days when she talked so much that her kindergarten teacher taped her mouth shut. This clearly was a bad idea by the teacher and, as you might expect, a somewhat traumatic experience for Mary.

"I truly never talked out loud in school until my sophomore year of college," she told me.

Communicating as a professional became a constant struggle, but one she eventually overcame.

"You have to do the hard things," she said. "If you speak in public twenty times, you're going to be better than you were. I found my own way. I feel like a lot of the way I navigated my college time and then my career involved figuring out how to communicate and relate with people that were different from me."

A common response by successful leaders to such fears and insecurities—or to injustice or bias, for that matter—was to speak out against them with truth rather than suffering in silence. For Denny Marie Post, for instance, a key moment in her career came when she simply said out loud that she wanted to become a CEO.

Denny was having lunch with Steve Carley, then the CEO of Red Robin, because he was looking for a chief marketing officer. She was qualified for the job and told him she could do it, but she wasn't interested in leaving her home in Seattle while her son was still in high school. She was ready to suggest other worthy candidates for the CMO role when she added, "Besides, I want to be a CEO."

Carley looked back at her and said, "Good, because I haven't got anybody currently in the organization who I believe could do that."

What she thought was a throwaway line ended up changing the course of her career. She and Carley mapped out a plan and stuck to it—she was CMO from 2011 to 2016 and held other roles of increasing responsibility, then was named president and CEO of Red Robin. Since leaving in 2019, she has been an advisor and board member to companies and organizations like the Women's Foodservice Forum, Vital Farms, Libbey, and *Travel + Leisure*.

"Giving voice to that ambition was a commitment that I made way too late," Denny told me. "I wish I'd done it earlier in my career, but when I finally did it, I found an advocate. And sure enough, we made it happen within the five-year commitment he made to me. So give voice to that and don't just wait for someone to recognize you, which is very much a female thing. You've got to raise your hand and take the risk. Having the courage to give voice to what you want to have happen and not be shy about it makes a world of difference."

Similarly, when others are hesitant to bet on you—or when they openly bet against you—Gerry Lopez and Angela Kleiman both suggested that you flip the script. Instead of asking yourself *why not?* ask them *why not?* And, as Gerry points out, be prepared with what he called a *why yes* response.

Gerry, who was born in Cuba, has a wide range of industry experiences, including roles as president of global consumer products for Starbucks, CEO of AMC Entertainment, and CEO of Extended Stay America. And he's no stranger to resistance from stakeholders, including many who focused on his ethnicity rather than the quality of his ideas.

When that happens, Gerry told me, you have two options.

"You can choose to focus on the negative," he said, "or you can choose to focus on the positive. You can choose to focus on all the barriers and you can choose to focus on all of the reasons why not, or you can choose to focus on the opportunities and the reasons why yes."

When others gave him reasons why they shouldn't do something, he was armed with *why yes* responses. If the *why not* arguments were legitimate, they might need to change their plan or course of action. But when he felt like he was being ignored or facing discrimination because of a bias against his Hispanic heritage, focusing on the business rather than the bias often allowed his *why yes* ideas to win the day.

"There's an opportunity in front of us," he would say, "and we can choose to make money with it, or we can just give it to somebody else. Because if we don't chase that opportunity, somebody else will and somebody else will get ahead of us. We can let biases or negativism get the best of us, or we can choose to be the better thinker—not because it's morally correct or politically correct. No, this is an opportunity. You can choose to make money with it or let somebody else get money with it. What are you gonna do?"

More often than not, the stakeholders did what was in their best financial interests and followed Gerry's lead. Sometimes, however, you have to drive a moral stake in the ground.

Angela, who was named president and CEO of Essex Property Trust in 2023, lived this out earlier in her career when she was in line for the role of chief financial officer and the organization's board initially wanted to give the job to someone who had never held a finance position. Her boss knew she wanted the job and deserved it, so he came to her with what he thought was a compromise.

What do you think about letting this other person be the CFO, even though you can call the shots? You're officially running the business, but the title would go to him?

In her own unique way, Angela told him why that was not a good idea: "I looked at him and said, 'Are you on crack?'"

Angela got the role and the title, but even when she was named CEO a few years later, she felt resistance from some quarters.

"Right after the announcement, it was a little rocky," she told me. "I will say the reception was not great. I was taken aback by how overt the bias was. I really didn't expect that. There were comments by multiple investors that questioned us about putting a female CEO in place. But you know, live and learn."

And don't give up.

"My biggest barrier was to muscle enough strength to keep moving forward, even though it didn't seem like it could materialize," she said of her career. "I had doubts about whether I would have the opportunity. Not so much about whether I could do it, but whether it was possible for somebody like me."

When opportunities came, she made the most of them by embracing a *why not?* mindset.

"My advice is to figure out what you're really good at and hone in on being the best in that, because that's how you can really make a difference," she told me. "From there, it's like concentric circles. Start building skill sets around your core competency, and if you can do that better than anybody else, then that becomes your competitive advantage."

And, she added, "Ignore the noise."

Why not?

DREAM CATCHERS

> Asking *why not?* as a rhetorical question is about having the courage to take risks and bet on yourself regardless of the barriers you face.

> Sometimes making a lateral move or taking a step back can put you on a path to somewhere better than you could have gotten by staying on your original course.

> Asking *why not?* requires an openness to move forward into uncomfortable waters and a willingness to at times be misunderstood.

> Taking risks and having ownership is a choice.

> ▷ You have to do the hard things to overcome your fears and insecurities as a leader.

> ▷ When opposition gives you a list of why you can't do something worthwhile, be prepared with a *why yes* response list.

> ▷ In the face of injustice or overt bias, be willing to drive a moral stake in the ground and speak up for what's fair and right.

QUESTIONS

1. What opportunities are you considering that require a *why not* response?
2. What ambitions do you have that you haven't given voice to?
3. In what areas do you lack self-confidence or struggle with fears, and how can you proactively face them?
4. What skill sets can you build around your core competency that can create your personal competitive advantage?

PRINCIPLE 3

FIND YOUR CHAMPIONS

The idea of the "self-made" success story is one of the great myths of modern times, and something the leaders I interviewed soundly debunked with their stories. It's true that we won't go far in life if we don't put in the work, and I'll talk in more detail about that in the next chapter. But no one makes it to the top—or even a few steps up the ladder—without some help.

Simply put: People need people.

Susan Stewart, for instance, never had a mentor, at least not in the formal sense, and a series of mostly bad bosses contributed to a rocky start to her professional career. Champions of her success, however, emerged along the way as she rose to prominence in the mortgage banking industry. And as was the case with so many of the leaders I interviewed, Susan's list of champions starts with her family.

Susan, who served as chairman of the Mortgage Bankers Association and is CEO of SWBC Mortgage in San Antonio, was a fifth-grader in Fort Worth, Texas, when her parents divorced. But while she called that her "first really hard life experience," her parents provided foundations in several areas that were critical to her success.

Her father, for instance, was a role model when it came to hard work and perseverance. He came from a hardscrabble background and took his first job when he was only nine years old. He worked his way through college and law school, ran the trust division of a bank, and oversaw a family foundation before retiring at the age of ninety.

"And my dad gave me all the good business advice," she said. "Be honest. Have integrity. Do the things that, no matter what's going on around you, you will be able to live with later. You know—just good advice."

Susan's mother, meanwhile, led by example when it came to embracing new challenges and giving back to others. When she found herself thirty-four and divorced with no work experience outside the home, she returned to college to finish the undergraduate degree she had abandoned when she got married. Then she added a master's degree in speech audiology and went to work in schools of low-income neighborhoods.

"These were children who had socioeconomic shortcomings or disadvantages and were treated as if they had learning disabilities," Susan told me. "My mother said, 'There's nothing wrong with these kids. They don't have a learning disability. They just haven't been exposed. Nobody has read to them. Their parents are working all kinds of jobs, and they just haven't had any opportunity to learn.' So she did that."

When she was around fifty, Susan's mom decided to go to law school and spent twenty-five years practicing family law.

By then, Susan was an adult in the workforce. Her parents, however, had instilled in her the belief that she, too, would get a good education and have a successful career. For the most part, in fact, she didn't grow up dreaming about things like going to college, having a career, or owning a home because, by the time she was a teenager, those were expectations.

"My dad grew up without really anything, and my mom grew up on a farm," she told me. "But my parents built our first house, and they built another house before they got divorced. So homeownership was embedded in my mind."

She finds it "painful," she told me, to think about kids who don't grow up with the expectation that they will succeed in school, work, and life.

"It was embedded in my mind that I'd go to college, and it was embedded in my mind that I'd be a homeowner," Susan said. "It was like that was just automatic. That's what happens in your life."

Interestingly, though, as a child she briefly dreamed of being a flight attendant, and her father bluntly told her she was aiming too low. Susan was taken in, she said, by a "really cool young woman friend" of her parents' who was a flight attendant and visited their home.

"I wanna do that when I grow up!" she told her father.

His response? *You don't wanna be a flying waitress.*

"Of course, that's insulting," Susan acknowledged. "They are a lot more than that. But the message I got was to shoot for something bigger, whatever that happens to be."

Figuring out what that would be didn't come quickly or easily.

"I thought maybe I'd be a lawyer, but I stumbled a little bit along the way," she told me. "After my parents split up, I just had a hard time and I ended up getting married really young, having children while I was in college, and then getting divorced really young. So I packed in a lot of trouble in my early years."

After she finished her bachelor's degree in business administration, Susan struggled to find any job with a professional career track. Prospective employers in the early 1980s would openly tell her, "We don't hire single moms. They're out all the time with sick kids." She eventually found a role working the telephones as a processor for CitiMortgage in 1983, not because she wanted a career in the mortgage industry but because that's the job she could get.

She earned a few promotions, mostly thanks to the support of her second supervisor, but a "series of not very good bosses" led her to an important conclusion: "I'm willing to do the work," she told me, "so I'm going to work for somebody who's going to support me in what I want to do."

After changing jobs a few times, Susan started a mortgage company for a custom homebuilding company in San Antonio. She had worked as an underwriter and an operations manager, so she had experiences that many loan officers lacked and avoided some of the mistakes young loan officers make.

Her business was growing when she got a call from Gary Dudley and Charlie Amato, who had founded SWBC as an insurance business about a decade earlier and wanted to add a mortgage division. They hired Susan to run it, giving her a relatively small budget but a great deal of freedom to make decisions.

In fact, that freedom was a condition for accepting the job.

"If I make a mistake, it's my problem," Susan told me. "I'll correct it. In fact, I have told them for years, 'If you ever have to come downstairs and tell me what to do, it's my day out of here, because that's not what I'm here for. I'm here to do it. I'm supposed to do and not have to be told.' So they allowed me to do whatever I thought was right."

In that regard, Dudley and Amato were champions by giving Susan the respect, encouragement, and freedom to build her part of the business, which she has done for more than three decades. SWBC Mortgage now operates in more than forty states and has around seven hundred employees. The company generates $3 billion in annual sales and has a servicing portfolio of more than $15 billion.

Susan's husband, Van Stewart, and her two daughters all work for SWBC, so they provide each other with support, and Susan also mentors younger leaders. She's grateful that she had people around her she respected and admired and could emulate, but she also is a big believer in formal mentoring.

"I wish I'd had a mentor, I'll just put it that way," she said. "I mentor these two young women now. One saw me on a stage and asked me if I'd do it. I said, yeah, I'll do it. Another one works in another part of the company. It's been every bit as impactful for me as it has for them."

MINING YOUR MENTORS FOR GOLD

Early in her career, Leslie Hale was visiting with one of her mentors when he posed a question that helped her reframe her view of her future: "Who are your peers?" he asked.

Her response began with the typical list—people she'd gone to school with, co-workers, and friends. But Alan Braxton, a founding member of the real estate investment firm Presidio Partners, was looking for a more aspirational answer.

Your peers are not the people who have the same background, came from the same neighborhood, or went to the same high school, he told her. Your peers are the people who are doing what you want to do.

"What he was trying to get me to do was look forward and to see myself as those people," Leslie told me. "He wanted me to see what they did and how they got there. It was probably one of the most profound questions that had been asked of me."

Mentors like Braxton had a profound influence on Leslie's life, helping her navigate challenges and opportunities as she rose to become the first African American female CEO of a publicly traded REIT in 2018 when she was named chief executive of RLJ Lodging Trust.

She sought the right champions in her life, and the rewards were significant. Braxton, for instance, introduced Leslie to Tom Baltimore, which led to her move from GE Capital to RLJ Lodging in 2005. There she worked with Tom, as well as with BET co-founder Bob Johnson.

"I was very strategic about who I was going to work with and why," Leslie said. "So having the chance to work with

Tom and Bob, it has paid off. I wouldn't be here where I am today if it wasn't for them."

Johnson founded the RLJ Companies—the initials are for Robert L. Johnson—while Baltimore, who also is featured throughout this book, was president, CEO, and director of RLJ Lodging Trust from 2011 to 2016, so he helped prepare Leslie to eventually move into that role.

"As I was looking for my next opportunity, I knew the number one thing on my list was people—somebody who was willing to open up about their experiences and to help me learn and grow," Leslie told me. "And I knew Tom was the right person for me to work with. Similar background. Similar work ethic. Both of us had something to prove, so to speak. And we had good spacing. He's ten years older than me, so it was easy for me to sort of tag along on his journey. And it turned out to be just an amazing experience."

Leslie typically worked on Saturdays when she first joined RLJ Lodging, but she switched her schedule and began working on Sundays because she knew that was a day when Tom would be in the office.

"When I came to work for Tom, I was only thirty-three," she said. "I was trying to be a sponge, and, you know, definitely absorb as much as I could. The most important lessons I learned from him were on Sundays. I would get ten to fifteen minutes with him, and I would pick his brain and ask him why he made certain decisions. What were you thinking? What did you mean when you said XYZ? I got an MBA on steroids from having the opportunity to work with Tom."

Tom no doubt appreciated Leslie's efforts given that he took a similar approach early in his career.

"I had one particular mentor at Marriott, and he was tough, rough, difficult," Tom said in a 2020 interview. "He worked six days a week and he always worked Saturday morning. I took it upon myself that no matter what I did on Friday night, I would get in early on Saturday mornings and prepare the analysis, the reports, or whatever he was going to look for."[1]

That mentor, Tom said, became a sponsor, not only helping Tom advance with Marriott but hiring him as a consultant while Tom worked on his MBA.

As a side note, Jodie McLean, CEO of the real estate firm EDENS, told me that early in her career she started her workdays at 5:00 a.m. because she knew she could meet at the coffeepot with founder Joe Edens and learn one-on-one from him about the investment business. Clearly, the strategy has some merit.

Leslie, meanwhile, told me she was always strategic about finding champions when she considered career moves, whether it was choosing Howard University for her undergraduate work because she sensed a nurturing atmosphere or looking for technical expertise at stops with GE and Goldman Sachs. And what she has needed from mentors has changed along the way, so she looked for different types of champions.

"When I was first starting out in my career at GE, my mentors were mostly white males," she said. "When I graduated from [Harvard] business school, my mentors were mostly Black males. When I moved into the C-suite, my mentors became predominantly women.

"Once I got to the C-suite, it wasn't about technical capabilities, which is what the first wave of it was about. It wasn't about how you navigate the politics in corporate America. I learned that in my second wave of mentors. It was really about how you lead as a woman in an industry where there are very few women, and particularly if you are an African American

---

1   Mandi Crisp, "A Conversation with Thomas J. Baltimore, Jr. (McIntire '85, Darden '91), Chairman, President, and CEO of Park Hotels & Resorts Inc.," University of Virginia, July 15, 2020, https://video.comm.virginia.edu/media/ A+Conversation+with+Thomas+J.+Baltimore,+Jr.+(McIntire+'85,+Darden+ '91),+Chairman,+President,+and+CEO+of+Park+Hotels+&+Resorts+Inc./ 1_5mriqz16.

woman. And how you operate in the C-suite when you're a parent, a wife, and all those things."

She mentioned leaders like Debbie Harmon (co-founder and co-CEO of Artemis Real Estate Partners) and Connie Moore (former CEO of BRE Properties and also featured in this book) as critical to her success at this stage in her career.

Connie, in fact, pushed Leslie to embrace the challenges of being a CEO, then gave her a unique and fitting memento to mark her promotion to chief executive: a picture of a ballerina's feet, one with a shoe on and one with a shoe off.

"If you've ever seen a ballerina's feet," Leslie told me, "you know they look pretty when they're all wrapped up, but in fact they are really damaged because of all the hard and painful work that goes into it. And that's the thing about why the women mentors were important in the back half of my career—they were uniquely positioned to understand the inherent struggles that I would face going through this role."

SUPPORT IN THE FIRES

Champions also can come in handy when you need someone to stand up for you, perhaps because you are under attack or perhaps because you need someone to sing your praises when you are up for a plumb assignment or promotion.

Clarence Otis, for instance, oversaw brands like Olive Garden, LongHorn Steakhouse, Cheddar's, and The Capital Grille when he was CEO of Darden Restaurants from 2004 through 2014, but he said the support of champions who were on the company's board were a key to his promotion to that role.

Perhaps the biggest of those supporters was Darden board member Odie Donald, a telecommunications executive whose roles included president of BellSouth Mobility and president of DirecTV.

"Odie pushed pretty hard because there was some reluctance that I think was predicated primarily on some people just not being that comfortable seeing a Black person in the CEO job," Clarence told me. "But the way it manifested itself was over whether I had enough experience operationally."

Clarence had served primarily in finance roles, including treasurer and chief financial officer. But Joe Lee, the outgoing CEO and another of his supporters on the board, had the foresight to suggest that Clarence spend time in general management as president of the firm's Smokey Bones restaurant brand. That experience was useful, Donald told his fellow board members, but it wasn't critical.

"Odie's point was, 'He's had some operational experience, but the key is the leadership team will follow him,'" Clarence said. "And when you looked around, I was who they expected to get the job."

While champions helped Clarence climb to the CEO chair, Daryl Carter got a lift from champions early in his career after he earned their respect by keeping his cool in a difficult situation.

Daryl, who now is CEO of Avanath Capital Management, one of the leading affordable housing firms in the country with more than $4 billion in properties across fourteen states, started out in the early 1980s in a real estate training program with Continental Illinois Bank. And he had been there a few months when he had what turned into an interesting and challenging phone call with a developer from Miami.

As they talked, the conversation turned to Daryl's background, so Daryl told him he had earned degrees from the University of Michigan and MIT and that he grew up in Detroit. This prompted the developer to express his opinion about the two biggest problems he saw with Detroit. One was that Detroit was too dependent on the auto industry. And the other was that there were too many Black people in Detroit.

The developer had assumed that Daryl was white. He's not.

"He used the N-word, and, of course, I was shocked," Daryl told me. "And he just went on about the N-word, using it several times. I didn't know what to do. I was just polite, got off the phone, and didn't tell anybody anything."

About a month later, two of Daryl's supervisors invited him to join them for a business lunch, and as it turned out, their other guest was the developer from Miami.

"We go to lunch and the guy sees me and I mean he freaks out," Daryl said. "He was like, 'Oh my God, you're Daryl Carter?' I said, 'Yeah.' And he said, 'We had a phone call.' And I said, 'Yes, we did.'"

I don't know if this is what the Good Book means when it refers to heaping burning coals on our enemies, but it seems to apply.

After lunch, the developer left and Daryl's supervisors began talking about how it seemed like something was wrong with the man. They went on and on about possible reasons why he was acting strange until finally Daryl said, "I think I know," and told them the story.

His supervisors apologized and "said all the right things," Daryl said, and once again he went on with his life.

Three days later, Daryl was summoned to the office of Jim Harper, an executive vice president and head of the bank's real estate lending division. Daryl arrived nervously at the meeting, partly because he suspected he was about to get a reprimand for violating the bank's policy of having an overdraft on his checking account. Harper didn't even know about that policy, he assured Daryl.

"Information travels fast," Daryl recalled Harper saying. "And I have two things to say. One, I know about what that person said to you. And, unfortunately, I can't promise that won't happen to you again in this industry. But what I will promise you that if you handle difficult situations with the class and dignity that you handled that one, you're going to be really successful in this business."

It was a great pep talk, but that wasn't the end of it.

Harper picked up the phone with Daryl in the room and called the developer.

"I'm here with Daryl Carter," he said, "and I understand you have issues with people of color. I don't want your business anymore. And if you walk into this bank again, I will have your ass thrown out on LaSalle Street."

Needless to say, it was a seminal moment in Daryl's journey.

"People don't do that," he said. "At that moment, if Jim Harper had dropped his shoes for me to shine every day, I would've happily done it."

But Daryl didn't just feel grateful. He also felt obligated to honor that support by excelling in his career as a way of honoring someone who had been his champion.

"This guy made a bet on me, and I was not about to mess up my career," he said. "This was someone that I was going to make proud, because he made a bet on me. That was eight months after I joined Continental Bank, and it was life changing for me."

That's what champions do.

DREAM CATCHERS

- ▷ No one is truly a self-made success; people need people.

- ▷ Champions are role models and advisors, sometimes informally and sometimes in formal, defined ways. They can be family members, friends, peers, mentors, or sponsors.

- ▷ If you aren't working for someone who supports you career aspirations, make plans to move into a role where the leadership will show you respect and help you grow toward your goals.

> ⟩ Learning from mentors and champions requires sacrifices and intentional effort. Coming to the office early or working on weekends can put you in a position to gain quality time with your champion. It's up to you to absorb what they have to share.

> ⟩ What you need from champions changes as your career and life progress. Look for help that fits your phase.

> ⟩ Your character—hard work, integrity, humility, and respect for others, for instance—often catches the attention of potential champions who will support you and stand up for you when you need it most.

QUESTIONS

1. Who championed your development early in your life, and what did you learn from them?
2. Who are your champions now?
3. Who are you strategically targeting as champions in the near future?
4. Who are your aspirational peers—the people who are doing what you want to do?
5. Who are you championing?

PRINCIPLE 4

MAKE WORK YOUR FAVORITE

There are really two types of people in this world: those who love *Elf*, the 2003 movie starring Will Ferrell, and who can effortlessly quote lines from it during almost any conversation, and those who, well...let's just say they are less enlightened when it comes to their tastes in Christmas flicks.

You can probably guess which camp I am in.

Elf is full of classic comedy scenes and classic one-liners like:

> ▷ "If you see a sign that says, 'peep show,' that doesn't mean that they're letting you look at the new toys before Christmas." (Santa)

> ▷ "This place reminds me of Santa's workshop except it smells like mushrooms and everyone looks like they want to hurt me." (Buddy)

> ▷ "As you can imagine, it's dangerous having an oven in an oak tree during the dry season." (Papa Elf)

It's not just great comedy, however. Intentional or not, *Elf* also offers a few pearls of wisdom.

For instance, when the manager in Gimbles (Faizon Love) asks Buddy the Elf (Ferrell) why he keeps smiling, Buddy says, "I just like to smile. Smiling's my favorite." To which the manager retorts, "Make work your favorite. That's your favorite, okay?"

What the manager doesn't realize is that it's not an either/ or proposition. Buddy ends up working all night to decorate the department store's North Pole area in anticipation of Santa's arrival. He makes work his favorite because it's work with a purpose, even if the real Santa doesn't show up and craziness ensues ("You sit on a throne of lies," Buddy tells the fake Santa).

The leaders I interviewed definitely don't sit on a throne of lies, but they have this in common with Buddy the Elf: They make work their favorite.

WORKING FOR CHANGE

Tom Baltimore, the chairman and CEO of Park Hotels & Resorts, was working his way through graduate school at the University of Virginia when he latched on to a phrase that accurately summed up his past while motivating him for the rest of his career: *If you want to change something, your level of dissatisfaction has to be greater than the cost of change.*

Reaching that level of dissatisfaction with the status quo, Tom realized, motivates you to willingly pay the price of creating something not only different but better. At that point, hard work no longer becomes drudgery but purposeful and therefore meaningful.

Hard work is a price for change and progress. And as a role model for hard work, Tom has few equals. But don't just look at the hours he puts into building a career; also consider *why* he puts in those hours.

For Tom, it starts with honoring his parents.

"My mother, more than anybody else, was laser-focused and had one dream and that was to see all five of her children—I'm the oldest of five—finish college," Tom said in a 2020 interview for a UVA McIntire Black Alumni and Student networking event. "She witnessed that. She preached education. She preached hard work. Those were real difference makers in my career. I think I'm the kind of man she would be proud of."[1]

Tom has worked hard in building a career in the hospitality industry, often in difficult situations. He helped lead one company through the aftershocks of 9/11 and during the Great Recession, and he guided Park Hotels & Resorts through the pandemic. He echoed what many industry leaders experienced when he said "there was no playbook" for that experience.

Tom's work ethic, however, applies to every aspect of his life, whether he's serving on boards, lecturing to business students at his alma mater, or giving his time to industry initiatives or nonprofit causes. He recognized early on that hard work was a key to creating a better life for himself and the people around him, because it was modeled for him while growing up in Montgomery County, Maryland, just outside of Washington, DC.

His family moved from rental property to rental property and never had much money, but work ethic always was attached to a higher purpose—self-improvement, serving each other, serving the community, and serving God (although not necessarily in that order). That's what his parents expected of Tom, because that's how they lived.

Tom's mother, Geraldine, took care of Tom and his four siblings but also worked nights answering after-hours calls for doctors' offices. And when Tom was fifteen, his father gave up a string of uninspiring jobs for something that paid even less—a calling to preach. At thirty-three, Rev. Thomas J. Baltimore Sr., founded The People's Community Baptist

---

1   Mandi Crisp, "A Conversation with Thomas J. Baltimore, Jr. (McIntire '85, Darden '91), Chairman, President, and CEO of Park Hotels & Resorts Inc.," University of Virginia, July 15, 2020, https://video.comm.virginia.edu/media/A+Conversation+with+Thomas+J.+Baltimore,+Jr.+(McIntire+'85,+Darden+'91),+Chairman,+President,+and+CEO+of+Park+Hotels+&+Resorts+Inc./1_5mriqz16.

Church in Silver Spring, Maryland, and went to work caring for his flock.

"It was a very challenging period because he went from making a very modest salary to no salary," Tom said in an interview with *UVA Today.* "He was an incredible servant, an incredible speaker. And he loved his work. It was his true passion and calling."[2]

Tom told me during our interview that he can't remember a time when he didn't have a job—delivering newspapers, washing dishes, or landscaping, for instance. But he worked equally hard in the classroom and also excelled as a basketball player. He played his freshman season at Baldwin Wallace College in Ohio but realized academics were his long-term ticket to success and transferred to UVA, where several of his friends attended.

The academics came somewhat naturally for him, he told me, but he had no safety net financially, so he felt constant pressure to excel in the classroom and with his part-time jobs.

"As a minority kid growing up and wanting to get ahead," he said, "I knew I had to be as good, if not better than others. I had to work harder. I didn't complain about that. I just accepted it."[3]

At Virginia, Tom earned a degree in accounting in 1985 and worked briefly for Price Waterhouse (now PricewaterhouseCoopers, or PwC) before shifting to the hospitality industry with Marriott Corporation. After earning an MBA in 1991, he continued with Marriott and then went to Hilton, where Bob Johnson, co-founder of BET, was a board member.

---

2   McGregor McCance, "Tom Baltimore: An Alum's Journey from Humble Beginnings to Corporate CEO," *UVAToday,* September 14, 2022, https://news.virginia.edu/content/tom-baltimore-alums-journey-humble-beginnings-corporate-ceo.

3   McGregor McCance, "Tom Baltimore: An Alum's Journey from Humble Beginnings to Corporate CEO," *UVAToday,* September 14, 2022, https://news.virginia.edu/content/tom-baltimore-alums-journey-humble-beginnings-corporate-ceo.

In 1999, Hilton added seventeen hotels through an acquisition. The Hilton leadership wanted to franchise and manage the hotels but not own them, and that provided an opportunity for Tom to partner with Johnson on a new venture. With Hilton's blessing and support (pre-Sarbanes-Oxley), Tom spent the next year working full-time for Hilton while also working with Johnson to form a private real estate investment company. And in 2000, they launched RLJ Development with ownership of seven of the hotels.

Tom was president and CEO of RLJ from 2011, when it went public as RLJ Lodging Trust, to 2016 before leaving to help start Park Hotels & Resorts, another independent spin-off from Hilton that now has a portfolio of more than forty premium-branded properties in cities like Orlando, Boston, New York, and Honolulu.

Along the way, Tom's reputation for working long hours, often coming to the office six days a week, was grounded in three guiding principles: prayer, preparation, and perseverance.

Prayer grounds him in gratitude and humility, he told me, which help prevent work from becoming his god. Preparation is where he most directly applies his work ethic—it's investing the time and energy to build good habits, learn information and insights, and develop relationships. And perseverance, of course, involves working hard through the inevitable challenges that come with life (like the pandemic).

Those principles have been key to his career success, but he acknowledges he has always struggled with work-life balance.

"I have admittedly failed in this respect," he said. "It is something I'm still working on."[4]

---

4   Mandi Crisp, "A Conversation with Thomas J. Baltimore, Jr. (McIntire '85, Darden '91), Chairman, President, and CEO of Park Hotels & Resorts Inc.," University of Virginia, July 15, 2020, https://video.comm.virginia.edu/media/ A+Conversation+with+Thomas+J.+Baltimore,+Jr.+(McIntire+'85,+Darden+ '91),+Chairman,+President,+and+CEO+of+Park+Hotels+&+Resorts+Inc./ 1_5mriqz16.

In recent years, he has begun playing more golf with his wife, Hilary, and their son and daughter.

"I have a reputation of working six days a week, and I still do," he said. "But my family is helping me work on finding that balance."[5]

THE STRATEGY OF HARD WORK

Tom's approach to work attracted like-minded protégés like Leslie Hale, who told me that sharing a similar background and view on work ethic was part of the reason she left GE Capital for RLJ Lodging Trust in 2005.

She, too, came from a family that modeled hard work—her parents owned daycare centers when she was growing up in South Central Los Angeles—and she, too, typically keeps a six-day work schedule.

"My work ethic is what drives me and differentiates me even today," said Leslie, who has been CEO of RLJ Lodging Trust since 2018. "Since I can remember, I worked six days a week, just as my parents did as entrepreneurs. That's what you do. Everybody says they want to be an entrepreneur, but they don't really understand what it takes. I saw it firsthand and so that work ethic I think I got from my parents."

She, like Tom, works those hours in very purposeful ways. For instance, when she was an undergraduate student at Howard University, she often was the first person to show up at the library, even on Saturdays, because that allowed her to do other things later that she enjoyed.

---

5   Mandi Crisp, "A Conversation with Thomas J. Baltimore, Jr. (McIntire '85, Darden '91), Chairman, President, and CEO of Park Hotels & Resorts Inc.," University of Virginia, July 15, 2020, https://video.comm.virginia.edu/media/ A+Conversation+with+Thomas+J.+Baltimore,+Jr.+(McIntire+'85,+Darden+ '91),+Chairman,+President,+and+CEO+of+Park+Hotels+&+Resorts+Inc./ 1_5mriqz16.

"My strategy was to do my work before I went to the football game," she told me. "Then when I was at the football game, I was having a good time and I wasn't worried about my homework. I was watching the band, and at Howard, you would watch the band. You don't watch the football game."

After college, Leslie said she typically worked five days for the company and one day for herself.

"That's always been my strategy in terms of reading an extra book, looking at an extra model, going the extra mile," she said. "On Monday, I was a little bit sharper and a little bit smarter. I guess part of the thing that drove me was I didn't feel like I belonged, so I always had to prove myself, and I always had to work harder and smarter just to fit in and to be recognized."

DEVELOPING EARLY HABITS

Everyone I interviewed shared stories that illustrated the importance of hard work, most of them learning it from their parents, and for Lili Dunn, the president and CEO of Bell Partners, the lessons came particularly early.

Lili's father, a fighter pilot in World War II, became a developer and residential real estate broker in upstate New York, and her mother was a professional ballerina. Lili was just eight years old when her mother died, leaving her and her brother to help manage the house while often tagging along with their father on business.

"Starting at a very young age, I was expected to cook dinner five nights a week, clean the house, get good grades, and be an athlete," she said. "There was no tolerance for excuses or to feel sorry for myself."

She recalled a story from when she was nine years old and her father was hosting a business dinner at their home.

"I came out with a huge platter with a leg of lamb," she said. "I remember everyone staring at me. At the time, I thought it was strange—*why are they looking at me so oddly?*

Now I understand. You don't see many nine-year-olds cooking a six-course meal for an adult dinner party."

By the time she was thirteen, Lili was already helping her father in his real estate office, attending some meetings, and visiting his developments. She was one of the youngest people to get her real estate license in Michigan, and at eighteen she began selling houses and leasing apartments, eventually starting a market survey business while in college.

"I learned very quickly how to be a survivor," she told me. "I had no safety net. No one to pay my way or console me when life threw me a curve ball. I stayed positive, never gave up, looked forward, and learned the value of hard work. I feel grateful and joyful for what I have achieved and for my family and friends. Although very difficult at the time, these challenging experiences shaped me into who I am today."

DON'T BE A DOORMAT

Connie Moore was twenty-five years old and wondered at times if she might have a heart attack from the stress of working long hours in an era when no one talked about work-life balance.

"One of my bosses said, 'You're a doormat. You never say no to a project,'" Connie remembered. But she didn't see it that way. As long as she was learning—and not having a heart attack—she was happy.

"I didn't have children, so I could work six and a half days a week," she said. "And I have my entire life. I started working when I was fifteen, and until the day I quit on April Fool's Day 2014, I worked six and a half days a week."

Connie, who now stays active as a member on several boards in the real estate industry, spent forty years working full-time, including nearly twelve years as CEO of BRE Properties, a REIT based in San Francisco.

"For me, it's not work," she told me. "I love what I'm doing. I don't know that I worked harder than the men. I just wanted to take on more because to me it was just more interesting. So I never thought about it as 'Oh, God! I'm just working so hard.'"

THE COMPETITIVE ADVANTAGE

One of the subthemes in stories of the leaders I interviewed was the competitive advantage they found in taking on tasks that others shied away from and simply working harder than other people.

As Belmont Village Senior Living founder and CEO Patricia Will told me, there are plenty of people with natural intelligence, but "if you don't combine that with some kind of drive and work ethic, it could all be for naught. It has to be both."

Susan Stewart, CEO of SWBC Mortgage, pointed out that there are times, especially early in a career, when the work really is drudgery, but that's okay if you have the understanding that doing it well will lead to something better.

"Be prepared to have to earn your way," she said. "I used to tell my daughters when they first were getting jobs that it doesn't matter if you like the job, it only matters if they like you. So quit telling me what you don't like at work, because if you don't like it, it doesn't really matter. You're not that valuable yet. Here's the deal: If they like you because you're doing a good job, you'll get promoted and eventually you'll like your job. You gotta put it in perspective."

A willingness to work hard, according to Realty Income President and CEO Sumit Roy, actually goes hand in hand with seeking help from others, because demonstrating hard work inspires others to help you in your career.

"Never be afraid of rolling up your sleeves and doing the hard work," Sumit told me. "Nothing in life will come if you're not willing to put in the hours and put in the effort. There are no shortcuts to success, but don't feel like you are in this world by yourself. There are plenty of people around who want to help, genuinely help, but you need to recognize those moments and you need to embrace those moments and take that first step to make those things happen."

DREAM CATCHERS

▷ Hard work isn't always fun, but it can be meaningful and enjoyable if it's connected to a worthwhile purpose and personal passions.

▷ Dissatisfaction with the status quo is a great motivator to work hard to change things for the better.

▷ It's not enough to work long hours; you need to work hard toward the right things and in the right ways. Hard work is more valuable and productive when done with a positive, no-complaining attitude.

▷ Successful leaders might not always outwork the people around them, but they almost always work so hard that they believe it's their competitive advantage.

▷ Hard work comes easier and more naturally when you do things you find interesting, but there's also a payoff to doing work that seems like drudgery if it leads to better opportunities in your career.

QUESTIONS

1. Who helps you strike the right balance between time spent on work and time spent on other worthwhile endeavors?
2. How is personal growth and development incorporated into your approach to hard work?
3. What tasks are you willing to take on that others shy away from so that you can apply hard work and gain a competitive advantage in your career?

PRINCIPLE 5

GET BACK UP

Leslie Hale grew up in a family that she describes as "entre-preneurial" and "middle class." Her father worked in the insurance industry, and her parents owned a daycare business, so it can sound pretty idyllic.

When you dig a little deeper, however, you begin to discover the source of the resilience, perseverance, and drive to succeed that helped Leslie become CEO of RLJ Lodging Trust and the first African American woman to lead a public real estate investment trust.

Leslie's grandparents were sharecroppers in Tennessee before they migrated to California, and her father, one of twelve children, built his career without a college education while living in South Central Los Angeles. Leslie had a stable family life, but she went to public schools where drug use, teenage pregnancies, and high school dropouts were the norm.

"There were plenty of opportunities to become a statis-tic," she told me. "I wanted to get out of Los Angeles by any means necessary."

Fortunately, she had parents who helped her see "that there was more to life than what we were seeing around us" and who helped her develop the skills and character traits to deal with the inevitable setbacks and disappointments that came her way.

When times got tough and she felt like she didn't belong or like it would be easy to give up, Leslie simply remembered where she came from and what her parents taught her about perseverance.

"I tried being poor and didn't like it," she told me. "I didn't want to go back to that, so I had to succeed."

Leslie experienced setbacks throughout her career, but one of her biggest professional disappointments, she told me, came in 2016 at a point when by all measures she already was successful. She joined RLJ Lodging Trust in 2005 and she was the CFO when Tom Baltimore, one of her mentors, stepped down as CEO in 2016. That's when Leslie was named chief operating officer, while the role of president and CEO went to Chief Investment Officer Ross Bierkan.

I asked her how she handled that.

"Not well at first," she said. "Not well."

Not getting that job, she told me, was a profound experience because it led to a period of self-discovery during which she had to ask tough questions and make important decisions.

"What are you gonna do about it?" she asked herself. "Are you gonna let it sour you? Or are you gonna take the opportunity and learn and grow? You have to decide how you will deal with situations when it all doesn't break your way and recognize that there are opportunities in situations like that if you remain calm. I mean, I still had great sponsorship on the board, even though I didn't have the role, and I had a team that respected me even though I didn't get the role. And so I really had to take stock."

Leslie didn't turn bitter but continued to work hard in the roles she was given, and two years later, she was named CEO.

"I took the opportunity to learn and grow," she said. "And I am appreciative today that I didn't get the job the first time. I'm a better executive and a better leader because I didn't get the job the first time."

Leslie said dealing with setbacks like not getting the promotion or having a business deal go the wrong way is difficult but in different ways than when dealing with setbacks that are more directly connected to gender or race.

"There's a moment of crisis in confidence, and you have to really learn to deal with a different kind of adversity," she said. "When you deal with adversity that has to do with gender and race, you can rationalize that because it happens every day. It happened to millions of people before me, and, sadly, it's going to happen to people after me. But when you have situations where you didn't get a job or where a transaction didn't go well or you had a business failure, developing a process and the ability to push through those moments is critical. Some people cut and run. Some people fold. They fall down, and they never get back up."

Hale's advice for getting back up is simple: Acknowledge it and move on.

"Whatever it is that you're dealing with, it's gonna loop in your head," she told me. "You will keep thinking about what you could have done differently, how it didn't go right—blah, blah, blah! So one of the things I do is sit down and write down everything that went wrong and what I could have done differently. Everything. And some things that went right. And once I do that, it's out of my system. I can look at it. I can agree with it. And then I can move on."

DOUBLE RS

Gerry Lopez did well in sales and marketing and worked his way up in organizations like Procter & Gamble, PepsiCo, and Starbucks, but at times he found himself in line for a promotion only to be told he was lacking some particular qualification or experience.

When he interviewed for the CEO role with AMC Entertainment, for instance, he was told by the private equity firm doing the search that he had two strikes against him: One, he had never been a CEO, and two, he lacked experience overseeing a company's financial statements.

As the consummate salesman, Gerry convinced the investors that every CEO had a first time to be a CEO and that the private equity firm could manage the balance sheet—which they knew they were going to do anyway—and he would manage the company.

He got the job.

Later, he was under consideration to become CEO of Extended Stay America, which offers mid-price extended-stay rooms in more than 560 hotels across forty states. This time he was told his CEO experience was a plus, but he lacked experience in the hospitality industry and didn't know anything about running a real estate investment trust.

He got that job, too.

Gerry, who was born in Cuba and raised in Puerto Rico, knew this from a lifetime of selling products and services: You hear the word "no" a lot in life. But he told me his simple "double R" strategy for dealing with that word.

"Resilience and results," he said. "Don't let the bastards get you down. And then produce the results."

Without resilience, you might never get the chance to produce the results. And without the results, resilience won't matter much. Together, as Gerry's career attests, you can have a broad career in consumer goods, food and beverage, retail, entertainment, and hospitality.

OVERCOMING FEARS

As a Jewish girl and the daughter of immigrants, Lynne Katzmann always felt like an outsider while growing up in a mostly Italian Catholic community in northern New Jersey.

"I think I was imbued with resilience, with the ability to find solutions to what seemed like very difficult problems, and also with a good deal of fear," she told me. "If you look to what shaped me, it's the ability to overcome fear, to be resilient, to accept opportunities, and to have grit."

For Lynne, who founded the senior living company Juniper Communities in 1988, getting up started with facing her fears.

"It's interesting when you talk about barriers," she said, "because fear can be traumatizing and it can be motivating, and I think at different times in my life, it was both."

For years, Lynne wrongly assumed her parents were born in America, but she knew her grandparents had escaped Nazi Germany, and the horrors of the Holocaust haunted her to the point that she, like Anne Frank, "always had a hiding place."

Lynne was a smart child, but the anxiety over not fitting in and her fear of Nazi oppression kept knocking her down when she was in grade school in the 1960s. Then she went to summer camp, and a counselor inspired her to get back up.

"I went to Y camp, so there were people of every color, but all girls," Lynne said. "I had a wonderful camp counselor, and she basically gave us a kind of confidence that I didn't have. And I came back that fall and just said, 'Screw it. I'm good with who I am.' I put together my own little group of people and went off and did all kinds of cool things."

For instance, she and her friends made their own movie about the ecology in their area.

"That was seminal for me," Lynne told me, "because it allowed me to come out of my fear and move ahead, and to take my differences and to not see them as negative or positive, but to be okay for what they were."

She began to find inspiration and strength in role models like her camp counselor, her grandmother, and a female German scientist who lived in their town.

"When I got to high school, there was nothing I couldn't do," she said. "I just had fun, and it was great. I didn't really care what people thought about me. I played lots of instruments. I did well in school. What I didn't do well in, I found something else to do. It was just fun."

She carried that mentality with her to college and into her business career, and it became a key to facing the inevitable barriers with resilience.

"There are always barriers to business, whether it be money or people or business cycles or global pandemics," she said. "I think the most significant barrier I faced was one from within. And if there's a message I could give, it's that you need to look within for that strength and you need to work with other people to build your experiences and connection. But ultimately, that strength, that resilience, that ability to look for solutions when very few appear to be there, is extremely important."

Given that advice, it's not surprising that Lynne named her company Juniper after the ubiquitous tree that is known for its ability to survive in harsh conditions.

"They're resilient, they're survivors, they're evergreen, and they represent the life spirit," she said of juniper trees. "If you're going to form a company that serves older adults and you believe that older adults are people who are not just waiting to die, then you look for an image that makes sense."

LESSONS FROM THE PANDEMIC

The leaders I interviewed all work or worked in industries that were hit particularly hard by the global pandemic. When you are investing in or managing businesses like restaurants, hotels, shopping centers, and senior living centers, few things will knock you down like the need for customers and employees to "shelter in place."

Tom Baltimore, chairman and CEO of Park Hotels & Resorts, led companies through the aftermath of 9/11 and through the Great Recession, but in July 2020, he called the pandemic an "extraordinarily difficult period" that was "really many times worse than both of those combined."[1]

Challenges like 9/11, however, helped leaders like Tom, Patricia Will, and Mit Shah create bonds within their teams that gave them confidence for every challenge that has followed.

"We had seven hotels under construction, and we had just bought three," Mit told me when describing the impact of 9/11 on his company, Noble Investment Group. "We had commitments out everywhere, and we didn't know what the future would hold. No one really knew what the future would hold. And the shock and the sadness that came as human beings also was followed with financial repercussions in our business. We never missed a loan payment, but it was a situation where I was concerned about whether this company could continue to meet its obligations."

Mit recalled arriving for work the next morning at 7:00 a.m. after a sleepless night and finding his entire team already there. They hugged each other, offered encouragement, committed to their future together, and began sorting through their options.

"I remember walking out of that meeting on September 12 knowing that we had something really, really special," Mit said.

He wasn't sure if it was going to be enough, he told me, but there was something powerful about knowing he had a team that cared for each other deeply and would pull together much like a family.

"I think that led to me being emboldened by the power of the possible," he said. "It gave me amazing amounts of courage to not only get through that time period, but to take really

---

1   Mandi Crisp, "A Conversation with Thomas J. Baltimore, Jr. (McIntire '85, Darden '91), Chairman, President, and CEO of Park Hotels & Resorts Inc.," University of Virginia, July 15, 2020, https://video.comm.virginia.edu/media/ A+Conversation+with+Thomas+J.+Baltimore,+Jr.+(McIntire+'85,+Darden+' 91),+Chairman,+President,+and+CEO+of+Park+Hotels+&+Resorts+Inc./ 1_5mriqz16.

measured risks about how we were going to think about the business, grow the business, and take advantage of something that I thought was our real secret sauce—our team."

Whether they were knocked down by 9/11, market recessions, or the pandemic, Mit said that team was the key to getting back up and fighting through the challenges.

"Every crisis was different," he said. "But the thing I continue to go back to is that who you go through life's journey with does matter personally and professionally."

For leaders in senior housing like Patricia Will, the founder and CEO of Houston-based Belmont Senior Living, the pandemic presented unique challenges because the company had to figure out how to support more than four thousand residents and more than four thousand caregivers rather than how to operate without them.

"It was the inverse of what everyone else was experiencing," Patricia told me. "Like everyone, we figured out how to run the company from home offices. But at the communities, we had to keep and encourage and cheerlead our staff through this extraordinary time. We had to become proficient in communicating with families every day. And we had to be at the hip of the greatest scientists to try to understand what we were dealing with and how to address it."

With more than thirty locations across the US and Mexico, Belmont's properties had been in the paths of hurricanes, fires, and other natural disasters over the years, but unlike those types of crisis events, the pandemic was sustained.

"We loved our people like never before, and I spent a lot of time in communities," she said. "I wasn't hiding, even long before I was vaccinated. And it was really remarkable to see how effective we could be. But it was antithetical to everything we do. We're in a business where you come to community, not only for the delivery of care, but for the engagement with other residents. Here, you go to a time where everybody stays in their apartments."

During the pandemic, Patricia found herself in a position where it was critical to help others as they struggled through a difficult situation, but she also knows that sometimes too much help can actually work against us.

When we get knocked down, we can draw strength and inspiration from others and perhaps draw on their direct help, but we also benefit from doing our part to get back up.

In 1987, for instance, Patricia and her husband both were in industries that were rocked by the financial crisis. Patricia was working for Mischer Development, a firm founded by the legendary Texas banker, real estate developer, and political kingmaker Walter Mischer Sr. As a partner in several deals that didn't go well, Patricia found herself responsible for a significant debt to the IRS. Her husband, meanwhile, was a young executive in the hard-hit energy industry.

"We were kind of hitting rock bottom," she told me. "We had a young family, and we both were working full-time and nothing was working. The bill that I got hit with from the IRS was more than our net worth, and I was indemnified by the partnership that I was part of."

While she never got any money from that partnership, she and her husband persevered and made it through. Then a few years later, after she had left the Mischer firm, she received a deed in the mail for a piece of property from Walter Mischer Sr. She called his secretary thinking it was a mistake, but she was assured that her former employer was perfectly lucid.

"Well, he owed you the money," she was told. "But he wanted you to make it through without the crutch." The deed to a random piece of property still came at a very welcome time, but by then they had made it through the worst of their financial troubles.

WHEN YOU KNOCK YOURSELF DOWN

Denny Post's career was repeatedly getting knocked down by her own behaviors, but for years she didn't even know it.

Denny, whose career in the restaurant industry included three years as president and CEO of Red Robin and more recently as co-president of Nextbite, spent most of her youth in El Paso. Her father was "not just a social drinker but an at-home drinker," she told me, and she and her friends often crossed the border to drink in Juarez, Mexico, so drinking became a normal part of her life by the time she was fifteen.

"I dabbled in a lot of stuff, but alcohol was definitely my drug of choice," she told me. "And it's such an insidious one because it is so accepted. I mean, we went out drinking every day after work when I was young. That was nothing. The two-martini lunch was real. It was two glasses of wine, three glasses of wine."

She never considered it a problem, however, until she was thirty-two and leading focus groups around the country as a marketing consultant.

"I had developed a habit of drinking in my hotel room," Denny told me. "I guess I'd had a little bit much and it may have showed up in my performance. My boss and mentor, Diane Kissell, asked me if I'd been drinking that day, and I was caught up short because I thought I was so good at managing this."

To her credit, Denny recognized her "addiction was a real problem" and chose to enter rehab.

"I'm very proud of my accomplishments—of my ability to work, my ability to succeed—and I was at risk of losing all that," she said. "A lot of people have a much deeper bottom. I had the threat of a bottom, which was losing my job. And that scared me enough. Frankly, they [her employers] were supportive enough for me to be able to go and do a rehab, but I've never looked back."

She's been sober, she told me, since 1989.

"It set me on a path of real clarity and health and honesty that made everything in the rest of my life possible," she said. "Marriage—I've been married for thirty years—having a child, having a career. It brought clarity to my life and a level of confidence that I just hadn't had."

FINDING RESILIENCE IN FAMILY

So, where do you find the courage and conviction to get back up?

Well, there's no one answer to that question, but many of the leaders I interviewed told me they drew strength and inspiration from parents and grandparents who endured setbacks and persevered.

For instance, Denny's mother was the daughter of a prominent politician in Warsaw, Poland, when Germany invaded her country. She had grown up with a governess, but at eighteen she became part of the underground resistance.

Denny's mother saw her father arrested and taken away, never to be seen again. Her sister was imprisoned at Auschwitz, the complex of concentration and extermination camps in German-occupied Poland, while she ended up in a prisoner of war camp before gaining her freedom and marrying an American army officer, Denny's father.

Her mother restarted her life in America, only to go through a traumatic divorce. But she bounced back from that, earned two college degrees, and had a successful career into her eighties as a bookkeeper.

"The core of my resilient heart is from my mother, because my mother had just a series of dramatic setbacks in her life and she always rose above it," Denny said. "She was really my role model, not just for how you bounce back, but how you grow from situations."

When jobs didn't work out for Denny, her mom was always there to proclaim something better would come along. And it did.

Jodie McLean, the CEO of EDENS, drew similar inspiration, but from her grandmothers.

"My story actually starts with my grandmothers' stories," Jodie told me. "I happen to be the granddaughter on one side of an immigrant woman whose husband just dropped dead when she had five- and three-year-old children. She was relatively uneducated and had to raise these two kids and use education, first for herself and then for the kids, as a way forward."

Jodie's other grandmother, meanwhile, had two young children when her husband was paralyzed by polio during World War II.

"They had no male counterbalance at that point," she said. "They were no nonsense, they were compassionate, they were gritty, they were savvy—they were courageous feminine warriors who were never stripped of their dignity, their humor, their pride."

DREAM CATCHERS

> ▹ Remembering how you faced and overcame trials earlier in life can help you deal with the inevitable new setbacks in life.

> ▹ Setbacks can lead to self-discovery if you ask yourself tough questions, keep an open mind, take personal responsibility, and learn from the experience.

> ▹ When you deal with a setback, examine what went well and what went wrong, and then move on.

> ▹ Resilience and results are a recipe for bouncing back from setbacks.

▷ Accepting yourself for who you are breeds self-confidence to take on challenges and not get discouraged by failures.

▷ Surrounding yourself with a good team and focusing on doing the right thing for the people around you will help you navigate difficult situations in life and work.

QUESTIONS

1. Who are the role models in your life when it comes to resilience and perseverance? What is it about them that you respect and admire, and how can you emulate those qualities?
2. Who in your life, personally and professionally, supports you through your most difficult trials?

PLAY THE HAND
YOU'RE DEALT

Daryl Carter was a sophomore at the University of Michigan when he approached a professor after an engineering class ended and asked a question about the day's lesson. The professor listened, but to Daryl's disappointment, it was not with an empathic ear.

"I don't remember exactly what he said," Daryl told me. "But it was like, 'Well, I'm not sure you belong here.'"

The comment shook Daryl. He knew how to take criticism, even extremely harsh criticism, but he wasn't expecting what seemed to be racially motivated animosity from one of his professors, and he wasn't sure how to handle it.

Daryl grew up in inner-city Detroit during the 1960s and 1970s, the son of working-class parents who had migrated from the South. His father worked primarily in the auto industry, which brought together a melting pot of ethnic employees, many of them immigrants. While the neighborhoods around the auto plants catered to different ethnic groups, the families from those groups frequently mixed for social events. And if they didn't have social ties, as Daryl noted, "union solidarity trumped race."

He also attended integrated schools at a time when Detroit's economy and the education system were much stronger than they are now. Neither of his parents completed high school, but they valued education. And from a young age, Daryl and his siblings visited the library every Thursday, checked out a book, and read it within a week. He developed a love for reading and he was a good student—so good that his parents insisted he take a bus to a more academically rigorous high school than the one closest to their home.

Daryl also excelled in sports, primarily basketball—he's six feet, eight inches tall. But while he was one of ten athletes from his high school who earned an athletic scholarship at the University of Michigan, he considered himself a "tag along" with the other, better athletes. He knew hard work and a good education would be the keys to his long-term success.

Daryl majored in architecture and while he didn't play much for the basketball team, he excelled in the classroom. That's why he found the professor's comment so disturbing. Daryl didn't know all the answers, but he was confident he belonged at the University of Michigan. He just wasn't sure he wanted to stay there. So he went home to discuss the matter with his mother.

He told her what happened, that he thought his professor was a racist, and that he figured his best option was to transfer to another college. But if he thought he would find sympathy from his mother, he was quickly corrected.

"No," she said, "you shouldn't do anything."

"Well, I don't know what to do," he told her.

"Just don't tell him you're Black," she said.

Daryl was smart enough not to sass his mother, but he remembers the thought that passed through his head when she gave him that advice: "I'm like, what in the hell do I do with that?"

Her motherly intuition must have kicked in, because she elaborated.

"It's his issue, not yours," she said. "Don't make it yours. Do what you need to do."

The message was consistent with the way Daryl's parents raised him, and it stuck with him throughout his academic and professional career.

"I guess I learned from an early age that whatever barrier there is, you have to figure out how to get around it, through it, over it," he said, "and not get as focused on whatever the impediment is. Just focus on getting around it or over it."

Daryl returned to class with the mindset that his best revenge was to work hard and earn the best possible grade. He interacted with the professor and continued to ask questions, but he didn't take the professor's responses personally. He believed that if he worked hard, he would be fine, and that proved to be the case. He passed the class, completed his bachelor's degree at Michigan, and then went to MIT for a master's degree in architecture and an MBA.

Daryl continued to face barriers to his dreams, although most of them, he said, weren't related to his race. And no matter the challenge, he focused on what he could do and not on someone else's issues that were beyond his control.

"I've learned that you don't obsess on people where you have pushback because you can't take it personally," Daryl said. "And there are many reasons that people may not like you. It may be because of the color of your skin. It may be the fact that they don't like tall people. It may be that their personality type just doesn't match with you. But there are many reasons, and I don't always go to the racial one first. I go to other reasons. So I think that was what I grew up with—that mentality of just not letting others define who you are."

The approach worked well for Daryl. His first postgraduate job with Continental Bank in Chicago launched a commercial real estate career that's lasted more than four decades. Daryl co-founded Capri Capital Finance and Advisors in 1992 and helped it build more than $8 billion in real estate equity value. Then in 2008 he founded Avanath Capital Management, a California-based firm that acquires, renovates, and operates apartment properties, with an emphasis on affordable and workforce communities. Since its inception, Avanath has acquired more than $4 billion of properties across fourteen states.

Daryl has a straightforward way of summarizing his approach to the adversities that naturally come in pursuit of high goals: Play the hand you're dealt.

"It's like playing poker," he told me. "Everybody's dealt a different set of hands. It's not the hand you're dealt, it's how you play it."

It's worth noting that Daryl learned the game from a statistics professor at MIT who was banned from the casinos in Las Vegas.

"Statistically, most people lose money in poker because they don't throw in enough bad hands," Daryl said. "But the great thing about poker is it keeps going around. So you have a bad hand, you throw it in. You lose a little money, but you're going to get a new hand. How well you play the bad hands defines what you're going to win more so than how well you play the good hands."

DO SOMETHING ABOUT IT

David Kong, who started his career as a dishwasher and busboy and would become president and CEO of BWH Hotel Group, took a similar approach. Instead of dwelling on the bad hands life dealt him, he adopted the mindset that "one door closes and another opens."

David's parents fled Communist China in the 1940s, and he was born and raised in Hong Kong before arriving at the University of Hawaii in 1970 with a one-way ticket, very little money, and no friends or family for support.

"From a young age, I realized that life may not be fair," said David. "So what? Do something about it."

What you do, of course, depends on the situation and the stakes involved. There are times when a battle isn't worth fighting, like with Daryl Carter's professor, and other times when you need to appropriately take a stand.

Connie Moore, for instance, built a career in finance and real estate investments, eventually becoming president and CEO of BRE Properties. She often was the only female senior leader in high-level meetings, and she faced more than her share of difficult barriers. Once when she was her firm's only female managing director, her boss took her to lunch and told her the firm was thinking of holding its annual meeting at a men's club in Chicago.

"How would you feel about that?" he asked.

"Are all of our shareholders men?" she said.

"Well, no," he said.

"Then that might be a problem," Connie told him.

They didn't hold the meeting at the men's club, but, Connie said, "I didn't make it about me. I've never made it about me. I've never made it about being female."

Diane Batayeh faced similar challenges on her way to becoming CEO of Village Green, which manages apartments and mixed retail space. She preaches patience when bad hands come your way, like when she felt she was passed over for promotions that were given to less-qualified men. But she also acknowledged she had to stand up for herself in the middle of an airport to get the attention of her new boss—and a promotion to vice president.

"I had never done that before," she said. "I'd always been very patient, but I'd had it because I had been looked over once again. And he was so taken aback by that—well, obviously I got what I wanted. But I never wanted to get it that way. I just fought for myself for the first time, and that's how I ultimately broke free from the whole perception of *I can only go so far, I can only be so much*."

Diane said standing up for herself earned her boss's respect, but she also said she had to earn the right to speak up in that way.

"I think people will push you and see how far they can go, how much they can get away with," she said. "And there's a time and there's a place for speaking up. I think you have to first prove your value before you demand your value."

PERSPECTIVE BIRTHS PERSEVERANCE

Perseverance is born of a correct perspective. You are less likely to persevere if you don't believe in yourself or if you are focused on negative aspects of life such as how others are treating you or how unfair life might feel.

Daryl first learned this lesson when he was about eleven years old and his mother bought him what he thought was the ugliest winter coat ever made.

"I was ridiculed even by my siblings," he said. "I hated this coat."

Winters in Detroit, of course, can be brutal, so it wasn't like he could go without wearing the coat. And he was wearing it the day he went to the corner store to spend the money he had earned from his job delivering newspapers. Daryl walked in thinking about which types of candy he would buy, only to discover two men were robbing the store at gunpoint. So he obediently got to the floor and prayed he wouldn't lose his thirty dollars.

He was right by the door as the robbers got ready to leave.

"Give me your money," one of them told him.

Daryl dejectedly began to hand over his money when the other robber intervened on his behalf.

"No," he said. "He's got to wear that coat. His family's doing worse than we are.'"

And they walked out.

"They didn't take my money," Daryl said, "and it was the happiest moment you can imagine. Well, I had a different perspective of that coat. You might say that was a negative that I had to wear that coat, but I felt so blessed that that coat saved me."

Like David and Daryl, many of the leaders I interviewed discovered that the hands some would view as bad were actually winners if viewed and played with the right attitude.

Connie Moore, for instance, was just out of high school when she went to work in the accounting department of a savings and loan. Her job as a part-time file clerk was about as mundane as it gets, but she didn't see it that way.

"I convinced myself that I was the most important person in the department," Connie told me. "I knew I needed to file everything super accurately because if I misfiled something, then somebody couldn't do their job."

Daryl, meanwhile, was a Black man in a mostly white working environment, but he said that helped him stand out when building relationships. People remembered him in part because he was different.

"I remember in the early days of going to conferences being the only African American in the building," Daryl said. "People would remember me."

Sometimes, he said, people would confuse him with Victor MacFarlane, another successful real estate leader who happens to be Black.

"I would say, 'No, I'm Daryl Carter. I'm taller, better looking. Victor is richer,'" Daryl said. "People would feel badly that they made that mistake and everything, but I would just counter it and say, 'Hey, that's great that you think I'm Victor, because I wish I was as rich as Victor.' And I would play it off and not be offended by it."

Connie had similar experiences when she began her involvement in industry associations.

"I walk into these organizations, and I'd be the only woman," said Connie. "So if you would volunteer to be on a panel or whatever, you knew they'd remember you, right? You either did good or you did bad, but they remembered you."

BUILDING A STRONG HAND

A big part of playing the hand you are dealt, the leaders told me, is simply embracing your strengths rather than worrying about your weaknesses, real or perceived.

David Kong, for instance, viewed his lack of charisma as a challenge early in his career but eventually learned to embrace the parts of his personality that were strengths rather than lamenting his weaknesses.

"I found out that I didn't need to try to be charismatic, but I needed to leverage my humility and patience and become a thoughtful leader, not a charismatic leader," he said. "I learned how to deal with head trash, the negative self-talk."

This type of self-awareness allows you to look for what you can do to improve a situation rather than blaming others or giving up.

When Daryl and Quintin Primo started Capri, they initially struggled to find an equity partner to help them launch the business. In fact, they pitched their idea fifty-seven times before they got a positive response.

"I would have to tell you, the first five we were very bitter," Daryl said. "Then I think around our sixth meeting we had someone who felt sorry for us and who just sat with us and took apart our pitch and said, 'You could focus more on this, and you could focus more on that.' It renewed our approach. And rather than being negative about a no, we used each no to get better at our pitch."

Daryl realized the "no's" weren't personal, and the only way to get to a "yes" was to learn and get better. He kept tossing in the bad hands for better cards—not the luck of the draw, but the aces that come with hard work and perseverance toward excellence. That's a hand that's hard to beat.

DREAM CATCHERS

- ▷ Don't allow other people's issues to become your issues. Focus on what you can do, not on the issues that hamstring others and are beyond your control.
- ▷ Don't let others define who you are.
- ▷ How well you play the bad hands in life often is more important than how well you play the good hands.
- ▷ A mindset of "one door closes and another opens" allows you to look forward to opportunities rather than dwell on the past.
- ▷ Playing the hand you are dealt can include standing up for yourself when others aren't playing fair. There's a time and place for appropriately speaking up, and if you've proved your value, people will listen.
- ▷ The hands some would view as bad are actually winners if viewed and played with the right attitude.

QUESTIONS

1. What bad hands have you been dealt, and how are you dealing with them?
2. How have you found that your perspective on your circumstances shapes your perseverance when dealing with those circumstances?
3. What strengths can you embrace to build a better hand regardless of your circumstances?

BUT DON'T SETTLE

Jodie McLean was sitting quietly in an economics class during her senior year at the University of South Carolina and day-dreaming about her future when the professor asked for her input on the topic of his lecture.

We've all been there, haven't we? Physically in a room with a group of people, yet mentally some place far, far away. Jodie had no idea what the professor had asked, so she did what any of us would have done.

"Excuse me," she said. "Can you repeat the question?"

The professor could have obliged, but he asked a different question instead.

"Excuse me," he shot back. "Why don't you tell me why you didn't hear me?"

Jodie knew she should have been paying attention, and she could have just apologized with the hope that he would ease off and get back to the subject at hand, whatever that happened to have been. But she was no shrinking violet in such situations. So she answered the question.

"Honestly," she said, "I'm sitting here and I'm thinking that this is the fall of my senior year and I'm going to graduate with distinction this year, and yet I don't have a clue how commerce happens. I know how to run the time value of money, and I know supply and demand. But I don't really know how business is created."

Jodie was playing the hand she was dealt (Principle 6), but she also was living out an important flip side to that principle—playing the hand you're dealt doesn't mean you have to settle for whatever comes your way.

Jodie regularly embodied the "don't settle" principle on her way to becoming president and CEO of EDENS, a South Carolina-based family-owned real estate firm that she helped grow to a national presence (with assets today valued at more than $6.5 billion). But it wasn't always easy, and she didn't always care for the hand she was dealt. She even gave in a few times—very few—but she seldom settled. She just adjusted.

In fact, Jodie was sitting in that economics class in South Carolina as a result of a concession to her parents. She grew up in Chicago, went to prep school in Connecticut, and had never been south of the Mason–Dixon line before graduating from high school. The University of South Carolina was never at the top of her list of college choices. Indeed, it wasn't even on the list.

Her mother, however, wanted Jodie to experience a large public university, and her godfather just happened to be the president of the University of South Carolina. When Jodie's father agreed that she should go there, she relented, headed south, and played the hand she was dealt—all the while expecting to transfer after a year.

It worked out well, of course, in part because she made the most of it. She embraced the new cultural experiences and received a high-quality education. And when it seemed she was getting less than what she wanted or needed, like the idea that she might finish her degree without really understanding how commerce was created, she spoke up about it.

There's tremendous opportunity, as leaders like Jodie will attest, in admitting that you don't know something and asking others for help figuring it out.

Thankfully, the professor wasn't about to let her settle, either.

"I think that's a brilliant thing for you to be thinking about," he told her when they met after the class. "How about if I put an independent study program together for you on entrepreneurship? You'll have some reading, and you'll go out and meet with entrepreneurs."

During that independent study, Jodie met Joe Edens, the founder of EDENS. And when she graduated in 1990, Joe asked her to join his firm full-time as an analyst.

"I said no," Jodie recalled. "I really wanted to go back to Chicago."

Jodie previously had done a summer internship in Chicago with a sports agency, which was a career she was interested in pursuing. The owner of the agency had advised her to go to law school or spend time in the financial sector first, and she could do either or both in her hometown of Chicago. The economy at that time, however, wasn't great, and her father convinced her to take a different path.

"I think you're crazy not to take that job for two years," he told her. "Just take it for two years and then you can go back to school. Get some stability with your first job and then you can relocate."

Jodie took the job with EDENS and never left the company. She hasn't always lived in South Carolina—she was in the firm's offices in Washington, DC, the day we spoke—but she has a home in Charleston, South Carolina, that's typically the gathering place for family events. She never pursued a career as a sports agent but instead found her calling in real estate.

"I was a finance major, and I just sort of fell into real estate," she told me. "As I continued into the real estate path, there were multiple moments when I had opportunities to step away from EDENS and pivot to do different things. And I will tell you at each moment I really sat and thought about the why. *Where am I going? Why do I want to go there?* And it always pushed me to make this place what I wanted it to be or create the opportunity that I needed. One opportunity always led to another, and I have no regrets."

Jodie was named EDENS's president in 2002 and CEO in 2015. It was under Joe Edens's mentorship that she learned how to balance her rational, hard-charging, goal-focused mentality with the art of knowing when to trust her emotions, when to slow down, and when to back off. But it was a balance, not a total shift. When she needed to stand firm, she stood firm.

In fact, Jodie's career almost got knocked off track early on, and it probably would have if she'd been willing to settle for less than she deserved. She had been working at EDENS for about five years when the president of the company came to her office to give her a pep talk that didn't turn out the way he had planned.

The president told her he was impressed by how hard she was working and the impact she was having on the company, so that was a good start. Then he said he knew she was going to have a great career as an analyst. She would do well and love it, he promised. Then he began explaining how they were bringing in a recent graduate from Duke's MBA program to run the firm's asset management group.

Jodie couldn't see the glass ceiling, but she knew it was there.

"He did not see anybody but a man in that role," Jodie told me. "And there was nobody but men in our most senior ranks at EDENS. I'm not sure if I saw myself there or not, but I certainly didn't see myself as an analyst forever. And I certainly saw myself as somebody who's continuing to evolve."

At 5:00 a.m. the next day, Jodie met Joe Edens at the coffeepot in the office and handed the company's founder her resignation letter. She didn't know where her career would take her, but she was going somewhere that didn't end where it started.

"Someday I'm gonna sit in a chair that looks like yours," she told him. "Somewhere. Probably not here. But I need to keep growing."

Edens took a more enlightened view of Jodie's potential than did the company's president, and he was quick to spot the opportunity in the situation.

"I've got this property in Florence, South Carolina," he told her. "I think it's the best property we own, but it's bleeding like none other. If you can redevelop that, I'll let you do whatever you want to do in the company."

They cut a deal on the spot, and as she was walking away, Jodie confirmed what she considered the most important part: "I'm in charge of the Florence mall—as in totally in charge, and I can make all decisions?"

Edens confirmed the agreement.

"Then my first move," Jodie said, "is to fire EDENS."

Edens, as you might imagine, gave her a quizzical look.

"Mr. Edens, it is obvious that no one out there except for you believes in me," Jodie told him. "And you've already told me they don't believe in this piece of real estate. So if nobody believes in me and they don't believe in this real estate, how am I going to impact change?"

"Okay, we're fired," he said. "You're on your own. Go do it."

That's when reality set in for Jodie.

"I was very proud of myself, but then I realized I didn't know anybody in Florence," she told me. "I had no network. So I turned around and I could see Mr. Edens with this huge grin, because he was probably the only person in the world who could stand me at that time. And I said, 'Mr. Edens, do you happen to know anybody in Florence, South Carolina, who could help me with the major redevelopment of this great asset?"

Edens smiled and handed her the business card of a real estate broker in Florence. Then Jodie and that broker formed a team that turned around the mall and, in fact, it did so well that it helped stabilize EDENS during a difficult financial time in the 1990s.

"I've had more significant projects since then," Jodie told me. "But when I look back, that's one of the most pivotal points of my career."

She refused to settle. And then played the card she'd been dealt.

GOING FOR *GANAS*

It's one thing to say you won't settle, but it's another to take the actions required to live out this principle. So how do successful leaders find contentment with what they have while avoiding the slippery slope of settling for something less than their full potential?

There's no one answer, of course. But Fannie Mae CEO Priscilla Almodovar referenced the Spanish word *ganas* during our conversation, and it struck me as a particularly powerful description of the approach I see in leaders who embrace the "don't settle" principle.

There's not really a perfect English equivalent for *ganas*, Priscilla told me. If you look it up, the word most frequently translates as *desire*. Turn it into a verb, *ganar*, and it also can mean *win*, *earn*, *gain*, *make*, *beat*, *profit*, *make money*, and the list goes on.

"It's like grit," Priscilla said. "But it's not just grit. It's a desire or a self-confidence where you know that even though you might not be the smartest person, you will somehow figure it out."

Priscilla recalled a debate with someone she described as a "know-it-all friend" about the difference between a "superachiever" and an "overachiever." Her friend, she said, fell in the category of a superachiever—someone who by their brilliance alone achieves far beyond what's normal. She, on the other hand, considers herself an overachiever—someone with the "basic smarts" who then excels beyond where those smarts could take her because of her *ganas*.

I know Priscilla well enough to say she brings more than "basic smarts" to the table, but there's no question that she has that something extra, that *ganas*, that has helped her go beyond what others might expect and never settle for an ordinary journey or self-limiting dreams.

Priscilla was the middle of three children born to parents who had moved to New York from Puerto Rico in the 1950s, and she learned her can-do attitude by watching their examples. Her father spent most of his career working in factories, while her mother went to college later in life and then taught school. They worked hard, saved their money, and created a better life for themselves and their children.

And it was clear early on that Priscilla had a bright future. When she was seven, Priscilla was using an attaché case rather than a book bag, perhaps an early indication that she would find her way into the corporate world. She went to public schools, first in Brooklyn and later on Long Island, graduated from high school when she was only sixteen, and enrolled at nearby Hofstra University.

Priscilla was a hard-charging economics major who joined every club on campus, got to know every professor, and was determined to take advantage of every opportunity that came her way. She made overpreparation a habit and was never afraid to ask questions.

"I got great grades," she told me, "but I worked really hard."

She was in Columbia Law School by the time she was twenty, not because she wanted to be an attorney but because she saw law as a flexible degree that could take her career in any number of directions. But in law school she began to experience some barriers she hadn't encountered while growing up in tight-knit Hispanic communities or while getting her undergraduate degree at a small private university.

Many of the other students represented the third or fourth generation from their families to attend Columbia. They had a polished aspect to their speech, not the clearly urban accent that Priscilla brought from Brooklyn and Long Island. And when she told a professor she had attended Hofstra, not Princeton, Harvard, or some other Ivy League school like most of her classmates, he dismissively said, "What's a Hofstra?"

Priscilla cried at times and thought the place was awful at the beginning, and she admits that she even began to downplay her Puerto Rican heritage. She had grown up extremely proud of her family and her culture—its food, traditions, and social bonds. At Columbia, however, many people assumed she was from Spain, and she didn't correct them.

"I'm not proud of this," she told me, "but I often share about it now."

She didn't allow the socioeconomic elitism to keep her down, however. With the encouragement and support of her parents, who were helping pay for her tuition, Priscilla doubled down on her efforts to overachieve in an academic environment that, as she began to realize, exposed some of the gaps in her education.

"I had some pretty fundamental stuff that I had to teach myself to do well when I was in law school," she told me.

And rather than settling for average grades, Priscilla soon "cracked the code," as she put it, for how to take law school exams.

"People think it's about writing beautiful prose," she said. "It's really all about issue spotting. There's no wrong or right answer. They just want to make sure you read the case and can spot the issues and come up with a logical argument. So in my second and third year, I just killed it."

Then she continued to "crack the code" in her professional career. She joined White & Case, a traditional law firm with very few women attorneys where her mentors were "quintessential Greenwich, Connecticut, white, patrician men." And at twenty-three, she immediately set her sights on becoming a partner. She learned the details of what was required to be a partner, created a plan, and went to work executing her plan.

"I always think like five years out," she said. "Let me just give it a try. So I gave it a shot, and I wasn't embarrassed about my aspirations."

The quintessential Greenwich, Connecticut, white, patrician men took notice, gave her stretch assignments, and judged her on her work, not her gender or ethnic background, she said. And she soon became an equity partner.

"I've learned that if you do good work and you raise your hand and are willing, people see that they can rely on you," she said. "And if you do what you say you're going to do, they don't care if you're a woman, Black, white, purple, or green. They just want the work done well."

When she married and had children, Priscilla decided the travel demands with White & Case were too great for her to excel professionally without sacrificing her family. So she left and began a journey that led her to the New York State Housing Finance Agency, JPMorgan Chase, and eventually Fannie Mae.

She didn't settle. She chose to prioritize what was most important to her—options where she could grow professionally and maintain a healthy family life.

Several times during our conversations, she mentioned that she was "very fortunate" to work for people who took risks on her and supported her career development, but of course, it's also clear that she played an important role. She earned their respect and she set her sights high, never settling for average. And with more-than-basic smarts and plenty of *ganas*, she continually overachieved.

DREAM CATCHERS

▷ Playing the hand you are dealt doesn't mean you have to settle for less than what you want from your life and career.

▷ If you don't know something that you need to know, don't be too proud to admit it or too afraid to ask others for help.

▷ When you consider options for you career, focus on the *where* and *why*—where you are going and why you want to go there.

▷ Refusing to settle often requires *ganas*—that unique combination of desire, grit, and self-confidence that propels you to figure out a way forward.

QUESTIONS

1. What actions do you regularly take to be content with what you have while refusing to settle for less than your full potential?
2. What ambitions do you have for five years into your future?

DO WHAT YOU LOVE, LOVE WHAT YOU DO

Amy Price loved her college experience, loved the work she did early in her career, loves her role as a wife and mother, and loves the work she does as president of BentallGreenOak (BGO), a global real estate investment company with around $81 billion in assets under management.

Her story, however, offers some counterintuitive insights about this grand idea of doing what you love and loving what you do. Often, it's less about deciding what you love and going after it, and more about a journey of self-discovery that takes you places where a love for your work becomes ingrained in your life.

"Success to me is the intersection of talent and passion," Amy told me. Arriving there comes from answering questions like, *What do you do well, and what do you like to do?* But there's no one path for finding those answers, she said, and the process takes more time for some than for others.

"There shouldn't be this expectation that there is one career progression and if you're not progressing this way then you are off track," Amy said. "As you develop a self-awareness and self-confidence about what you actually like to do and do well, you put yourself in a position to do that."

It's easy to look at successful leaders in any profession and focus on the bold moves they took along the way to achieve career success, but every leader I know took some wrong turns along the way or found unexpected passions and skills from paths they never intended to travel on. The more they learned during those parts of their journeys, the more their bold moves set them up to truly enjoy their work, even the more challenging aspects of it.

"You can be bold when it's rooted in self-awareness, self-confidence, and direction, but I didn't start out by being bold," Amy told me. "You have to do the work to figure yourself out. Be honest. No right or wrong. Just know yourself and *then* don't be held back. Be bold, one hundred percent."

This approach flies against the misguided idea floating around the universe that tells people they need to "find their passion" and once they do that, everything in life—personally and professionally—will settle into a state of nirvana.

Indeed, a passion for your work is vital to success—it's something I found in everyone I interviewed, something I've personally experienced, and something I've seen in the top leaders I've worked with throughout my career. But it's not something you find like a hidden gem in a cave or a pearl in the ocean. It's something, as Amy experienced, that you develop and fine-tune.

The discovery comes with a process, and while you might identify some of your passions early on in life, that process involves learning how to align them with your gifts and talents. Just because you have a passion for basketball, for instance, doesn't mean you have the talent to make a living in the NBA. And new passions can emerge with new experiences. Maybe something that initially seems like an "interest"—like math or finance—will develop into a passion when applied in the right career setting.

Most of the leaders I interviewed, for instance, didn't grow up dreaming of careers in real estate, finance, hospitality, or investments. And all of them had pivots in their careers as experiences and circumstances took them places where they hadn't expected to go but that proved vital to the type of self-discovery Amy mentioned.

Amy, perhaps more than anyone else I interviewed, eased into adulthood with a go-with-the-flow approach to life.

She grew up in a somewhat idyllic but sheltered environment in the suburbs of Los Angeles, where her father spent much of his career as a systems consultant with IBM, while her mother was a homemaker before teaching elementary school. And Amy made good grades with minimal effort in good public schools while excelling in gymnastics, softball, and volleyball.

But it was only in retrospect that she realized her passion for sports was rooted in a love for being part of a team and contributing to the success of her teammates—in other words, that it was all about the people. And her career ambitions weren't particularly laser-focused, either. Even her first significant life decision—where to attend college—was made without a great deal of serious thought for her long-term future.

"I was very happy I could go to college," she said, "but I was focused on the college experience and not the path it would put me on after four years."

Amy was drawn toward the idea of leaving California for "something different," and the photos she saw of Colgate University in a brochure "looked pretty." That was enough to get her on a plane to the East Coast to visit a few small private schools in Massachusetts, Connecticut, and New York.

"I got back and I remember my dad saying to me as we walked out of the airport, kind of joking, 'Where do I send the check?'" Amy said. "And I said, 'You can send it to Colgate.'"

Next thing she knew, Amy was on her way to Hamilton, New York, not because of its academic excellence, but because it just sort of seemed like the place to go. She figured she would attend Colgate for a semester and, worst case, if she didn't like it, she would transfer to UCLA or California-Berkeley.

"It was not well informed," she said of her decision. "It wasn't, 'Gosh, Colgate's good at this.' I went there—and I will say this is kind of an Amy theme—because I liked the people, I liked the community, and I felt like there was a nice balance. It's academic enough, athletic enough, and social enough, but it's also really about college. It's in the middle of nowhere, so you don't bleed into a city."

Amy told me she didn't exactly fit in at Colgate—after all, she was a Southern California kid who didn't know enough to buy boots with good treads for the snow and ice—but she was accepted and considered a bit of an interesting novelty as she slipped and slid around the campus during the winter.

"It was a great community of people," she said. "It was just very different, the antithesis of my high school, which was just what I was looking for."

So she stuck around and graduated magna cum laude with a degree in economics, again, not because she dreamed of a career in economics but because the "business world was interesting."

With no long-range goal for her career, Amy took a job as a financial analyst for Morgan Stanley thinking she would stay a couple of years and see where that led. And, serendipitously, it led to nearly twenty years with the firm and a broad range of experiences that introduced her to real estate investments and commercial mortgages, as well as REITs and corporate finance, all while working in New York City, Hong Kong, and San Francisco.

The more she experienced, the more she loved what she was doing.

Early in her time with Morgan Stanley, Amy paid her own way to business school because she wanted to increase her exposure to the options she had for her career, then she returned to Morgan Stanley to experience those options.

"In hindsight, what kept me at Morgan Stanley the most is that I felt supported, valued, and engaged by the people I worked with," she told me. "And again, I think I happened into it. But as I reflect back, I feel like choosing people is critically important to me."

When Amy told her boss she wanted to move to San Francisco so her husband, Garrett, would have greater access to grow his career in the venture technology field, she figured she'd have to leave Morgan Stanley, which didn't have a real estate investment team in the Bay Area. Instead, they put Amy in charge of developing a team and a business in San Francisco, and she became managing director and head of real estate investing for the western United States.

Morgan Stanley was "a phenomenal place" where she learned and always felt supported, she said, but after she married and began having children, she didn't see women who were role models for the type of life she wanted. It struck her that the top-level female executives showcased by the firm as successful career women were either unmarried with no children so they could devote their full attention to their careers, or they had children and a stable full of nannies to help take care of them.

Neither of those approaches were bad. They just weren't for Amy, and that created a bit of a conundrum when it came to her career growth.

"There was probably a three-to-five-year period in there after I had my first child where I really just took it year by year," Amy told me. "And I think that was critically important in hindsight because the idea of knowing where I wanted to be in ten years was just too overwhelming. I didn't know, and I didn't feel like I saw the path. So there was a period of time where I told myself, 'Amy, you don't have to figure it out forever. Just figure it out year by year.'"

This wasn't an approach she broadcast to her peers or bosses. She was in an environment where she felt like everyone else had aspirations and direction, and she didn't want to create the perception that she wasn't "all in" when it came to her work. In her mind, however, she could be all in without creating self-imposed pressure about her future.

Eventually, she felt ready for a change, and by now she knew more about what she loved to do, what she was good at, what she valued, and what she wanted for her future. She could be bold within the context of greater self-awareness. So in 2012, she joined Bentall Kennedy, the Canadian real estate investment firm that later merged with GreenOak to form BGO.

Amy had met Mike McKee when he was CFO of the Irvine Company and she was early in her career with Morgan Stanley, and she had been impressed by how he handled his work and the way he led people. McKee had gone on to become CEO of the Irvine Company, then CEO of Bentall Kennedy US. Amy felt she could learn from him, and after meeting with him again, she knew he wanted her to succeed. She also wanted to do something different, something that offered room to grow, but not something entrepreneurial.

"I'm not a start-from-zero person," she said. "I am married to that person, but I am not that person."

Amy spent nine years as president and chief investment officer of Bentall Kennedy US prior to the merger. Now, as president of BentallGreenOak since 2021, she oversees all of the US and Canadian businesses and is a member of the global executive team, the management committee, and several investment committees.

It was a circuitous route from the suburbs of LA, but she ended up figuring out what she loves to do and is doing it. In many ways, I think she was living out something I read in a newsletter by author James Clear: "Before you discover what you love: fewer commitments, more experiments. After you discover what you love: fewer experiments, more commitments."[1]

SPACES AND PLACES

Leslie Hale looks back on her career and doesn't see any aspect of the journey that she doesn't use today in her role as president and CEO of RLJ Lodging Trust.

---

1   James Clear, "3-2-1: On Regrets, Failing Gloriously, and How to Make Good Choices," JamesClear.com, October 5, 2023, https://jamesclear.com/3-2-1/october-5-2023.

"All of those experiences play a key role in my decision-making capacity," she told me.

That's true because Leslie made the most of whatever experiences came her way, of course. But she also was more intentionally strategic than someone like Amy when it came to forging a path that exposed her to work that fit with her interests. Her path wasn't necessarily better than Amy's, just different; but like Amy's path, Leslie's approach moved her toward a better understanding of how to do what she loved.

Leslie went to Howard University in 1990, for instance, because she believed it was a place where she would be "nurtured," and, as it turned out, that's where she found her first love.

"It wasn't a person," she said. "It was finance. When I took my first finance class and I realized you could take a dollar and make it into two, I was like, *Wow, that's for me.* I really loved finance. I loved to think about it. I loved the fact that it was forward-thinking, analytical, and strategic."

Then when she was working at GE in her first role after college, she discovered her second love—real estate.

"It was really tangible, something that we experience every day in our lives," she said. "You touch real estate, whether it's a house you live in or hotel you stay in or building you work in. We all touch it. So I married it with my first love, which was finance—the numbers and the analytics."

What brought it all together for Leslie—and this was similar to Amy's story—was working with the right people and the right places where her interests and passions could thrive. It's an approach Leslie calls spaces and places.

"What I've always tried to do in my life and my career is put myself in spaces and places not where I could be successful but where I could be extraordinarily successful," she said. "That's a function of understanding what your strengths are and leaning into those. And it's a function of understanding the people you surround yourself with and the things that align with who you are as a person."

She found those spaces and places throughout her career, but nowhere more than at RLJ, where she worked with and for Tom Baltimore, a mentor and someone she credits with allowing her the space to flourish. Leslie joined the firm in 2005 and was executive vice president, chief operating officer, and chief financial officer before becoming president and CEO in 2018.

"One of the key things that has allowed me to be successful at RLJ is that I found the place that allowed me to be my whole self," she said. "I didn't have to worry about being a woman or an African American. It was an organization that embraced all of me."

People of color who can embrace their entire self, she said, can perform at a higher level.

"I think I was able to be extraordinarily successful at RLJ because all the baggage that many minorities face, I didn't have to face that here," she said. "I was able to focus on producing tremendous outcomes, and as a result, this is what I've been able to achieve."

FOLLOWING PASSION OVER MONEY

Alice Carr looked over the course options for her freshman year at Occidental College in Los Angeles, saw an advanced math class as an option, and signed up for it. She was majoring in American studies and German literature, mind you, so high-level math wasn't required. But she liked math and gravitated toward the most challenging classes possible.

"I remember cursing myself," she told me. "It was eight a.m. and I was going into the calculus class with all the math nerds who knew exactly what they were doing. I had taken it in high school, so I thought it was going to be a piece of cake, no big deal. It was really hard, but I loved it."

Those final four words—"but I loved it"—epitomize the lessons learned from Alice's story.

Alice, the CEO of April Housing, has never shied away from "really hard" in her journey. Not every opportunity turned out to be a perfect fit, so focusing on the positives—the parts she loved—helped her move toward what she believes she ultimately was meant to do.

During her junior year in college, for instance, Alice went to Germany for a study abroad program. At nineteen, she spent the first three weeks living alone because her host family showed her to her room and then promptly took the stipend they'd been paid and went on vacation. She called it a "character-building" experience.

Later, she did internships with a nonprofit community development corporation in South Central Los Angeles and with the LA housing department. Then after earning a graduate degree from UCLA, she moved to San Francisco and spent "five years of hard-core rolling up my sleeves" for an under-resourced community development financial institution (CDFI) that made loans to affordable housing projects.

All those opportunities aligned with her passions: first, immersing herself in a foreign language and culture, then later, helping make the world better by creating opportunities for affordable housing. But Alice's career took an unexpected turn when she was recruited by a bank that wanted her to help build a community lending group. She figured a couple of years in banking would look good on her résumé, so she took the job thinking she would soon return to the nonprofit sector. Instead, she found an unexpected path to doing what she loved.

"What I didn't realize was that the unlimited resources and the unlimited support of the bank to build out the department was intoxicating," she told me. "And it was really fun— the amount of work you could get done, the amount of loans you could make, and the team we were building."

Alice never returned to the nonprofit world, but she stayed connected to affordable housing as she moved into roles for Citi and JPMorgan Chase, enduring the Great Recession along the way. Today she runs April Housing, one of the biggest affordable housing businesses in the country.

"I believe in the cause of affordable housing," she told me. "Affordable housing is the linchpin of what makes a successful family and a healthy community. It is really what allows people to fulfill their potential through education and jobs. Having a safe and stable place to live is critical."

Alice grew up one of five children living within their means as a big family in an affluent community. As a child and young adult, she said "money was never really an issue," giving her the opportunity to freely pursue what she really believed in.

So she figured out her passion for affordable housing when she was in grad school at UCLA, then figured out the best ways to apply her gifts and talents to that passion, and that's what led to a successful career.

"Money wasn't my main motivator," she told me. "I always thought I would work at a nonprofit, and I would've stayed in a nonprofit if the resources had been better, honestly. I was able to accomplish so much more at the bank, and then that career just really took off.

"I never thought I would end up in the place I am today. I was motivated by the work and the sense of purpose. It sounds cliché, but to really find something that you can sink your teeth into and that you can really enjoy, that's not just work but also your interests, and brings them all together, I think that's what made me successful."

DREAM CATCHERS

▷ Doing what you love and loving what you do often involves a journey of self-discovery that takes you places where a love for your work becomes ingrained in your life.

▷ Incorporating your passions into your work comes during the process of identifying what matters to you and aligning those things with your gifts and talents.

▷ "Before you discover what you love: fewer commitments, more experiments. After you discover what you love: fewer experiments, more commitments." — James Clear

▷ Passions often thrive when they are put to use in the right places and with the right people, or what Leslie Hale calls "spaces and places."

▷ Focusing on the aspects you love about a task helps you push through the parts of it that are really hard.

QUESTIONS

1. In what ways are your talents and passions intersecting in your career?
2. How comfortable are you with taking a year-by-year approach to your career aspirations until you can solidify your long-term goals?
3. How intentionally strategic are you about mapping out your career and exposing yourself to areas of interest?

LIVE TO LEARN

Clarence Otis grew up in one of the biggest cities on the planet, and yet his formative years were typically restricted to just a few square miles in and around the Watts area of southern Los Angeles.

His mother didn't drive, his father worked two jobs as a janitor, and there was almost no public transportation in their part of the city. Gangs ruled the streets, and when Clarence was nine, police brutality triggered riots that left parts of Watts in flames and its stores ripe for looters.

In short, there was nowhere to go and no way to get there.

"We were confined to a very small community from a geographic perspective," Clarence told me. "So what you knew was well known, but it was tiny."

His parents, however, knew there was much more to the world than what their family could see and experience in Watts, and they were determined to expose their children to the possibilities that existed beyond the inner city. The exposure they provided became foundational to a journey that took Clarence places he could only imagine as a child, culminating in roles as CEO and chairman of Darden, the world's largest full-service restaurant company.

In the late 1960s, President Johnson's Great Society domestic agenda resulted in dozens of programs aimed at addressing poverty, and Clarence's mother signed him and his three siblings up for everything that came their way. They also were frequent visitors to the Watts Towers of Simon Rodia, which had an arts center that birthed a generation of talented Black writers and artists. And the family checked out as many books as possible each week from the neighborhood's public library.

"I used to read all the time," he told me. "That was the way to get exposed, to see the world through the eyes of the authors, fiction and nonfiction."

Clarence's father, meanwhile, was a former Marine who had fought in the Korean War before migrating west from Mississippi when Clarence was four. He had seen other parts of the United States and the world, and he knew the value of exposing his children to it.

For a period of about ten years when Clarence was young, however, his father worked two full-time jobs. The shifts overlapped, so he had no days off. He worked eight hours three days a week and sixteen hours the other four. Still, he did his part to show his children what life looked like beyond their neighborhood.

"On one of those three days when he only worked eight hours, he would bundle us all up in the car and just drive the city," Clarence told me. "That included driving through the higher end neighborhoods in the city like Beverly Hills and Bel Air. So that was some of the only exposure we got to what was going on outside the city until high school."

Clarence and his siblings didn't have many responsibilities as children, but they had one that shaped them for the rest of their lives: education.

"My parents expected us to do well," Clarence told me. "My father didn't see why, given that we had nothing else that we were responsible for, we couldn't do well in school. So the expectations were that we would do well, and we did."

By the time Clarence graduated from high school, more and more universities were desegregating, and he and his younger sister both went to Williams College, which is one of the most academically elite schools in the country. It also was about as far away from Watts as they could have gone—roughly three thousand miles to the northeast in Williamstown, Massachusetts.

Clarence, and later his sister, were among multiple generations of students who were recruited from the inner city to attend Williams College by Felix Grossman, an attorney in California and an alumnus of the school.

"There were five of us at Williams from the same inner-city Los Angeles high school [out of about 1,800 students]," he said, "so we were beneficiaries of that moment."

Clarence graduated magna cum laude and Phi Beta Kappa from Williams College in 1977, then went to Stanford Law School where he graduated in 1980.

"I guess my thought is that most of education is about how well you read and reading comprehension," Clarence told me. "So even if it's mathematics or engineering, and I took a lot of math classes at Williams, ultimately you have to understand the problem you're trying to address. You have to read and know the background. Being well read was the foundation for being able to do well academically."

Clarence began his professional career in New York as a securities attorney before entering the financial services industry. Then in 1995, he joined Orlando-based Darden Restaurants, which operates such chains as Olive Garden, LongHorn Steakhouse, Cheddar's, and Yard House. He began as the company's treasurer, was named CEO in 2004, and became chairman in 2005. Since 2014, he has spent most of his time serving on corporate and nonprofit boards.

Exposure through education and by getting involved in group activities (in school and later in industry) was critical to his success, he said, but not just to his rise to the top of the leadership chain. The thirst for learning—which starts with knowing you don't have all the answers—also helped make him a better leader at each stage of his journey.

"The more senior you get, the more you realize that you have to wait to weigh in," he told me. "Otherwise, all you are going to hear is your own point of view, because no one's going to really challenge it. And the key to leading is to get a contribution from everybody, and then hopefully what comes out of that is a point of view from the team that is effective and successful."

THE VALUE OF EXPOSURE

Sumit Roy grew up in India, which is very different from Watts, and began his college career at Georgia College in Milledgeville, Georgia, which is very different from Williamstown, Massachusetts. But Sumit, the president and CEO of one of the highest-performing REITs in the country (Realty Income), has this in common with Clarence Otis: They both emphasized the importance of learning everything they could by getting exposure to as much as possible.

Indeed, the word "exposure" came up over and over during my conversation with Sumit.

At Georgia College, Sumit says he was "exposed to hardware that I'd never seen before" and was able to learn how computers really worked. At the University of Georgia, where he earned his master's degree, he was "exposed" to more "incredible machines," a larger campus environment, and the opportunity to teach as a graduate student. And his first job after college was with a consulting firm, where he "really got exposed" to a professional environment.

"It was a completely different ball game, and in some ways it actually helped me accelerate what it was to be a professional," Sumit told me. "How do you carry yourself? What are the clothes you wear? How do you conduct yourself in business? All of that got accelerated."

The first client Sumit worked with was Bell South, so he was "exposed" to the telecommunications industry. Then he got an MBA from the University of Chicago so he could learn more about how business actually works, and that exposed him to the world of investment banking.

"I had no clue what investment banking was," he said. "Absolutely no idea."

He learned, of course, and that resulted in a job with the technology group for Merrill Lynch.

"I just felt at home because the more technical the analysis was, that's where I thrived," he said. "I got exposed to a lot of different businesses, and then the dot-com thing happened and it was a real hit."

In 2004, he was recruited to UBS to help augment a newly formed real estate investment banking team, which was totally outside his wheelhouse. But, again, he was eager to learn.

"Look, I know nothing about real estate," he told them.

"All we need from you is your technical skills, and we'll teach you the rest," they said.

For Sumit, that was a "marriage made in heaven," and indeed, the next seven years, from 2004 to 2011, exposed him to businesses and deals across the globe, sparked his passion for real estate, and provided a master class in leadership and investment strategies that set him up for the future.

"I got to meet some amazing senior management leaders while I was still at a junior level," Sumit said. "That exposure, again, just continued to help me create my own style by seeing what I deemed as being a successful trait to mimic or embrace. And that exposure, along with being exposed to many different strategies—seeing some that were successful, some that were not as successful—allowed me to formulate my own thinking around how a company is successful."

One thing Sumit learned was that he longed for a more stable environment, something a little less prone to boom and bust. With his wife's encouragement and support, he took a cut in pay in 2011 for a more balanced lifestyle with Realty Income, where he served as chief investment officer and chief operating officer before becoming CEO in 2018.

An enduring lesson from his journey, Sumit told me, is the value of keeping an open mind while exploring options and looking for the best solutions to whatever challenges he faced.

"I do think I have a contrarian mindset, not because I just want to be contrarian for the sake of being contrarian, but I don't necessarily feel like I have to follow the crowds," he said. "That mindset has been developed over time. It is so much easier to just follow the crowds, and that's an impediment. I've had to teach myself to recognize that you've got to believe in your independent thinking. Listen to everyone, but at the end of the day, you've got to make your own conclusions."

It's by continually learning and growing that he can develop the type of informed opinions that are valuable to his team and his clients.

"In investment banking, I realized that I was not doing my clients a good deed by just regurgitating what they can read in the newspaper or they can learn from when they pick up a research report," he said. "I believed in independent thinking and was confident to put forth my ideas, even at the expense of disagreeing with my clients. The moral imperative to provide my thoughts despite the associated controversy has not dissuaded me from speaking my mind and being truthful to what I believed was in the best interest of my client."

CLOSING THE GAP

Diane Batayeh's firsthand experience with the old maxim "you don't know what you don't know" helped spark her pursuit of a live-to-learn approach to life.

Diane, who was born and grew up in southwest Detroit after her parents immigrated from Jordan, was a high achiever and in the top 10 percent of her high school class, so she didn't lack for confidence when she joined students from across Michigan for a mock legislative session. But while learning more about how government functions, she was surprised to discover the distance she still needed to travel to compete on the bigger academic stage.

"That was my first glimpse of the vast difference between the other students' intellectual achievement levels versus ours in the inner city," Diane told me. "I became very insecure and very quiet. I didn't speak up, which was the opposite of how I behaved in my inner-city high school."

Diane, the CEO of Village Green Property Management since 2017, has had a long and successful career in the real estate investment industry, but she would not have predicted it after her confidence took a hit at that high school event. In fact, it took several years and a good bit of hard work to regain that confidence, but she did it by prioritizing her education.

Diane was one of seven children—six girls—and she was raised in a culture where the women seldom sought higher education or professional careers. Her father's idea of success for his daughters was that they would finish high school and marry someone "with really good health insurance," she said.

The reality check regarding where she ranked among the state's scholars easily could have caused her to shift her goals for life. Diane had good teachers in high school and they did their best, she said, but they were under-resourced. So when she considered her family's expectations and her experiences with the state's other top students, she almost passed on the opportunity to attend the University of Michigan.

That idea, however, didn't go over well with LeRoy Rowley, Diane's band teacher and mentor, and he encouraged her with some blunt advice: "What the hell are you thinking?" he said. "Get comfortable being uncomfortable. Get out. You have to go."[1]

She went. And she was uncomfortable.

---

1   Mary Salmonsen, Christine Serlin, and Symone Strong, "Multifamily Women of Influence," *Multifamily Executive Magazine*, April 13, 2021, https://www.multifamilyexecutive.com/business-finance/leadership/multifamily-women-of-influence_o?&o=2.

"That definitely was a very big challenge for me—having to go to extra study groups and working extra hard in college," she told me. "My first year of college was a huge struggle, just adapting and adjusting and not feeling smart, actually feeling quite the opposite. And that really can mess with your brain—the psychological impact of feeling like I was not properly prepared."

Her only option, as she saw it, was to work harder and close the gaps between what she knew and what she needed to learn. And her personal pride and a desire to prove herself to her parents motivated her to persevere in her academic career.

"I couldn't tuck my tail between my legs and go back and say, 'Gosh, I never should have tried,'" Diane said. "My parents didn't know about my struggles. They would not have understood. They would have said, 'Come home, you never should have gone.' So I really had to suffer in silence there, and I didn't have any other choice, right?"

It was as a student at Michigan that Diane took a part-time role in 1980 as a leasing agent for Village Green, but she had no idea that it would launch a career that's lasted more than forty years with the company. It was a family business at the time, and she had good bosses and bad bosses as she continued the trend of learning and growing along with the company, which now manages apartment complexes and mixed-use retail in around fifty cities.

"I took advantage of the opportunity to learn," she said.

When the company expanded to the West, Diane raised her hand to relocate to Denver and played key roles as she learned the development and investment side of the business. She returned to Detroit as chief operating officer; then, shortly after the family sold the business to Compatriot Capital, she became CEO.

"I never really had a plan to be the CEO," she said. "It was really just a matter of seizing opportunities and overcoming the fear of failing at something new."

That's the advice she consistently passes on to others, whether it's someone she's mentoring, someone she's teaching in the Village Green training program, or someone listening to her in an audience when she's giving a speech.

"You have to say yes to opportunities that may seem outside your realm of experience or outside your comfort zone," she said. "Saying yes takes courage when it's an unknown. It's so easy for us to stay inside of our comfort zone and do what we know we're good at. But it's very difficult to do something maybe you're not good at or maybe you've never done and take the risk of failing, because that's scary."

The courage to embrace the unknown and recognize that you don't have all the answers, she said, results in humility and requires a degree of patience so you can learn what you need to know before you take actions.

"What I've learned over time is you really don't know everything, and you're better off waiting if you're not sure than acting with limited information," Diane said. "You need the ability to zoom out and be strategic. That's very hard, because there is this pressure on the younger generation to be a vice president on Day One. There is an expectation, a social pressure, that you've got to be big—you've got to have something to post every day to be important and relevant.

"It's very difficult to be patient today, but you don't know everything and you want to avoid mistakes along the way. So take your time making decisions. Patience is extraordinarily important. I haven't always had it, but where I have, it's paid off."

THE POWER OF PREPARATION

Diane's message of patience might at first glance seem counter to something Debra Still told me during our discussion: "Doing something is always better than doing nothing."

Debra, however, was making the point about times of uncertainty when you have gathered all the information available and you need to make decisions and take action even though you know there are questions you still can't completely answer.

In other words, gather as much input and data as you can but realize that you can never know everything and that certain situations require you to rely on your expertise and good instincts. Then when it's time to make a decision, act based on what you know and don't give in to paralysis by analysis. And that perfectly aligns with what Diane was saying.

Debra spent nineteen years as president and CEO of Pulte Mortgage and now is vice chair of Pulte Financial Services, which operates mortgage and insurance businesses and has more than a thousand employees throughout the United States. She got there by taking decisive action, but those decisions were based on a commitment to preparation and to an inclusive approach to leadership.

"One of the biggest lessons I learned early in my career was to listen and not have strong opinions too early in any discussion," she said. "I learned to ask very probing questions. Have we thought about this? Have we thought about that? Instead of saying I think we need to do whatever. Asking probing questions really helps, because everybody becomes motivated to answer those questions and we ultimately hear all the voices in the room. I now sit on two public boards, and this approach has made me a good board member because I don't try to manage. I just ask the probing questions."

The questions she asks are informed by her preparation, and the answers she gets become additional data points that prepare her for making hard decisions or offering opinions.

Interestingly, that commitment to preparation originated in an unexpected place.

Debra was working on a graduate degree in finance at George Washington University, but it was a class on lobbying that had the biggest impact on her career by teaching her the value of preparation.

"My focus was on mortgage banking, and I just picked up the course because I needed the credit," she told me.

In this class, students were assigned topics—hers was the trans-Alaska oil pipeline—and spent the semester developing a political policy position that they would have to defend. Their grade depended on how well they sold their ideas to the class at the end of the term.

"What this experience taught me was that with enough preparation, I could become expert on any topic," she said. "That started giving me the motivation and ultimately self-confidence to put energy and research into learning what I needed to know to be successful. And as long as I've invested in enough preparation, I can pretty much do anything. That class also helped me have the confidence to speak to large groups, first at my company and ultimately within the industry."

That type of self-confidence was missing early in her life.

Debra, who considered herself a "modest student" in high school, grew up with a passion for sports, so she earned an undergraduate degree in physical education, health, and recreation and spent a year teaching physical education before moving to San Diego with her husband, who was in the navy.

Unable to land a teaching role, she took a job with a mortgage company during a boom period in the late 1970s. When her husband was transferred to the Pentagon, she figured she would return to teaching in the Washington, DC, area, but by then she had developed a love for real estate and mortgage banking.

That's when she enrolled at George Washington, but her education never ended. Instead, she built a career on studying the characteristics of strong leadership, noting the things she liked and didn't like about the leaders she worked with, learning from her mistakes, and taking in as much information as possible so that she would be prepared to be a strong leader.

"One of the components of leadership that I feel is very important is having a healthy level of curiosity," Debra told me. "I'm a naturally curious person, which is why I'm always learning."

That approach set her up for success whether she was leading the efforts to centralize Pulte's operations, chairing the Mortgage Bankers Association, or testifying on behalf of the industry during congressional hearings. But her curiosity required taking risks and going places others weren't willing or interested in going.

When she was working as a branch manager in Dallas, for instance, Pulte's leadership team asked every division to provide a participant in a program on total quality management. No one in Debra's division wanted to do it except for her, so she volunteered, not realizing the other thirty participants would be construction managers.

"It was all about manufacturing principles—you know, total quality and quality checks during the process," she said. "I was literally a mortgage banker sitting in the middle of a construction group, but they let me stay and I learned all about manufacturing principles and total quality management. Volunteering had led to a valuable experience and unique visibility."

Unbeknownst to her, several senior leaders in the company attended those meetings, and Debra soon realized that "making yourself visible" was also an important part of her career development. When it was time to pick someone to move to Denver and lead the efforts to reorganize the company, Debra stood out in how well she prepared, how eager she was to learn, and how effective she was in her other roles.

The move to Denver was a bit of a risk, since it involved making major changes to how the company was structured and trying ideas that were totally foreign to her industry. But she described that part of her career as "more fun" than scary.

"It let me reinvent mortgage banking," she said. "I'd been given a chance to take everything that was ineffective about the mortgage process and change it. We started applying manufacturing principles, workflow design, and process management. And I truly believe that if I had not taken that job, I would not have ultimately attained the role of CEO."

Even her worst moments, she said, helped prepare her for future successes.

"I feel very good about not wasting any of my experiences," she said. "For instance, one time an entire branch was recruited away by a competitor. I thought I had failed. I thought my career was over. But a wise gentleman told me it's not the problem you're going to be measured by, it's how you manage through it. And from that point forward, I've never been afraid of setbacks or difficult situations."

DREAM CATCHERS

> ▷ Living to learn involves regularly exposing yourself to new ideas by investing in things like diverse relationships, experiences, and reading (fiction and nonfiction).

> ▷ The thirst for learning starts with knowing you don't have all the answers.

> ▷ An open mind typically arrives at the best solutions to the most difficult challenges.

> ▷ Personal growth often requires that we get comfortable being uncomfortable—taking on stretch assignments and embracing life's hardest challenges.

> ▷ There's value in patiently gathering the necessary information before making important decisions, but

when you have all the information you can get, doing something often is better than doing nothing.

> Preparation leads to good questions that lead to diverse opinions that lead to better decisions.

> Learning from failures allows you to never waste an experience.

QUESTIONS

1. In what ways are you regularly exposing yourself to new things in life?
2. How is fear of failure holding you back from a worthwhile opportunity?

PRIORITIZE PEOPLE

Chris Howard and Mit Shah walked very different paths and achieved different versions of success, but I was struck during my interviews with these two men by the similar role that empathy has played in their stories.

We all want and need empathy from others, and it's great when we get it. Chris and Mit, however, didn't just talk about *receiving* empathy from others; they emphasized the importance of putting empathy into practice—a critical component to the principle of prioritizing people.

Empathy is a tough skill to master. It requires "the ability to share someone else's feelings or experiences by imagining what it would be like to be in that person's situation."[1] And as my friend Walt Rakowich points out, sharing someone else's feelings is "where empathy gets tricky." Regardless of how well we intellectually understand a situation or how much we try to imagine how a person might have felt, he said, we can't always know or feel what another person is going through.[2]

When we prioritize empathy, however, we nurture related skills like concern and compassion for others. We are less

---

1   "Empathy," Cambridge Dictionary, 2024, https://dictionary.cambridge.org/us/dictionary/english/empathy.

2   Walt Rakowich, "Rethinking Empathy: How to Share Support When You Don't Share Another's Experience," WaltRakowich.com, January 2023, https://waltrakowich.com/rethinkingempathy/.

judgmental and more forgiving. And we are better equipped to prioritize the people in our lives, even when—perhaps especially when—they seem bound and determined to make it hard. So even if we can't always truly empathize with someone, we can show a positive regard for their humanity and prioritize a healthy relationship with them.

This is what I see in the lives of Chris and Mit. And while they learned it in different ways, for both it was a by-product of the examples set by their families and the experiences they had in the formative years of their lives.

Chris, executive vice president and COO of Arizona State University, grew up in Texas with a strong connection to his family's heritage. His great-great grandfather, Amos Howard, was "an enslaved person" who lived to be over a hundred, Chris told me. And following the Civil War, his ancestors were mostly sharecroppers until his grandfather migrated to East Texas, landed a factory job, and started what Chris calls a "virtuous rather than vicious cycle" by modeling hard work and emphasizing education and service to others.

Chris's father, Marvin, was the first in the family to attend college, which is where he met Chris's mother. His dad also rose to the rank of captain while serving in the army in Vietnam before starting a career as an industrial engineer for Texas Instruments and UPS, where he became a senior manager.

Chris felt a strong sense of responsibility to honor his family's legacy, and he has clearly done that. He excelled as a student and athlete in high school, graduating twenty-first in a class of more than 1,300 students at Plano High School. He graduated from the Air Force Academy and spent eight years on active duty, including time with the Joint Special Operations Command and as a helicopter pilot. He earned a doctorate as a Rhodes Scholar at Oxford and an MBA from Harvard Business School, worked for Bristol Myers Squibb and GE, and was president of Hampden-Sydney College and Robert Morris University prior to joining the executive team at ASU.

Mit, meanwhile, is the son of Indian immigrants. His father came to the United States for college, eventually earned a PhD, and was working as a food scientist when the family decided to pursue their entrepreneurial dream. So they borrowed some money from family members and bought the Winkler Motor Inn in Winston-Salem, North Carolina.

Mit worked at the hotel from the time he was ten until he left for Wake Forest University, where he earned an economics degree. Then he took a job with a small investment firm in Atlanta, and with that firm's help and some money he borrowed from his parents, he soon launched the Noble Investment Group, where he is CEO and senior managing principal. Over the last thirty years, Noble has grown to more than $6 billion in assets, including investments in around two hundred hotels.

These quick summaries tell you something about the personal accomplishments of Chris and Mit, as well as a little about what motivates them. But they don't tell you much about how or why prioritizing people helped them build their careers, and that's where the stories of empathy and compassion come more sharply into focus.

LEANING INTO DIPLOMACY

For Chris, the earliest lessons about relationships came not only from his parents but from his experiences in school.

Chris and his brother started in an elementary school that was racially diverse and then went to one where the majority of the students were Black, but ended up in mostly white Plano, Texas, just north of Dallas. There he learned quickly how to remain comfortable with who he was, while connecting with people around him.

As a fifth grader at his new school in the 1970s, Chris told me he was involved in "a lot of fistfights" over "certain words that should not be used." But by the time he was a senior in high school, Chris was president of the student body, president of the Fellowship of Christian Athletes, captain of the football team, commander of the joint ROTC unit, and in the top fifteen of his class academically.

It helped that he was a star football player. As he said, "All sins are forgiven in Texas if you can play football." But adulation for gridiron stars often is superficial. Chris earned a deeper, more genuine respect because he worked hard to get to know people, learned to appreciate their stories and what mattered to them, and showed them the type of respect he wanted for himself.

"I was a diplomat before I knew how to spell the word diplomat," Chris told me.

Chris found a winning combination in remaining true to himself, excelling at the tasks he was given, and valuing and honoring the people around him. That wasn't easy, of course. Race, as he said, was a "multiplier or divider," not an "addition or subtraction" when he was growing up. At times he felt the sting of mixed messages—praise for his athletic achievements, for instance, along with subtle racial stereotypes.

"Living with that as a fifteen-year-old takes a lot of sensemaking and getting in your head sorting things out," Chris told me. "So that's the journey. That was the life my brother and I lived, but we made it through. We're okay."

Once he enrolled at the Air Force Academy, Chris became more fully conscious of the differences between himself and his non-Black peers. He was in many ways conservative in his thinking, but he was progressive on civil rights, and his views weren't always shared by others. As he began to develop a better understanding of his views, he also began to develop understanding, and at times empathy, for those who were different from him.

For instance, there was a cadet who freely and regularly used the N-word one evening during a card game with all white cadets. When this got back to the command structure, they held a conduct hearing to decide whether to let the student stay or send him home to Mississippi. The student wasn't expelled, however, and part of the reason was that Chris testified on his behalf.

"He grew up in a place where the white people lived on one side of town and the Black people lived on the other side," Chris recalled saying at the hearing. "And the reason I know that is because he told me. I think this guy has a good heart. I just don't think he knows what he doesn't know because he was using the N-word in front of white cadets and they were offended."

Chris wasn't defending the cadet's use of an inappropriate term, but he believed the man needed an opportunity to learn and grow.

Chris also learned that just because he had different views from someone white didn't mean those differences were driven by race. In a political science class he engaged in a debate with a cadet, who also happened to be from Mississippi, about an issue involving the NAACP.

"After class we were talking," Chris said, "and he says, 'Chris, I feel badly because you hear my accent and you think that I'm racist. I'm not racist. Listen to the comments that I made.' And I was like, 'You know what? You're right.' I was going after him, but he was not disparaging the NAACP. He was making a critique of the NAACP. He was just making an intellectual comment. And I had this point of empathy where I realized I was judging a book by its cover."

Chris learned that empathy was a perfect complement to effort.

"Effort and empathy are great, because you don't have to be a rocket scientist to do either one," he said. "You have complete control of your effort. You have complete control of your ability to try to put yourself in somebody else's shoes. Think about that. It costs no money. You don't have to be rich. You don't have to be smart. You don't have to be well connected or good-looking. You can just work hard and smart and then you can say, 'How would I feel if I were him or her?'"

Effort and empathy, he said, were cultivated in his life by the people around him, and those qualities then drew people to him who provided support and encouragement along the way.

"If you're willing to lean in an inch, there are probably thirty-five people who will help you pull forward," he said. "You've just got to be willing to lean in that inch. It's not always easy. It's not always going to be evident. But it is there, including for Black men and Black people. There's so much out there that people want to give if you just find a way to lean in with your best."

SEEING THE GOOD

Like Chris, Mit Shah credits his parents for their example of how to combine hard work with an appreciation for people and the importance of authentic relationships, even when others don't treat you as you'd like to be treated.

"I learned the power of people," Mit told me, "and that all experiences, good or bad, are formative."

Watching his father leave a stable job to be an entrepreneur created in Mit a deep appreciation for what it means to sacrifice for others, because his parents were sacrificing for the long-term good of their family. And working with them to build a business deepened his appreciation for the struggles and stories of all the people he encountered, whether that was his friends in school or the guests at their motel.

"My experiences from the time I was ten until I left for college provided me with a unique ability to develop empathy before I knew what empathy really meant," he said.

Mit's father, who came from rural India and attended college during the 1960s in Knoxville, Tennessee, and Logan, Utah, experienced his share of bias. And he taught Mit not to take it personally when he had similar experiences in life.

"Good people can act in ways that might not always seem good," Mit said. "But seeing the good in people is an important characteristic, no matter what your faith is, and there are ways to respond in those situations."

Because his parents chose the hospitality industry, Mit at times saw guests get angry, sometimes about legitimate issues and sometimes over minor incidents or about things over which no one had any control. Each time, his father had a choice about how to respond, and different responses, Mit realized, would lead to different outcomes.

This interested Mit so much that he minored in sociology at Wake Forest, where he added to his understanding of why people respond differently to different forms of communication or different tones of your voice.

Throughout college and into his professional career, Mit found that the better he got to know people and understand things like their communication style or the baggage in their background, the more successfully he could build a healthy relationship with them and support them in their goals for life. This idea of serving the people around him grew even more important as he launched and grew his business.

"Everybody has a dream," he told me. "One of the greatest joys I get is to help the people on my team fulfill theirs, and that creates an amazing amount of solidarity and loyalty for this journey that we're on."

In an investments-based business, Mit points out that access to capital and talent are essential, and both require that people trust you and believe in you. That requires strong relationships that are forged over time and that will stand the tests that come with adversity.

You might recall that in Principle 5 I shared how Mit's team came together in the days and weeks following 9/11. What he saw, in my opinion, was the fruits of prioritizing people. He had prioritized his team for years and developed compassion and empathy as shared values, so they were up for the challenge. As Mit put it, "Who you go through life's journey with does matter, personally and professionally."

HARMONIOUS DISCORD

Chris and Mit weren't the only leaders I interviewed who spoke directly or indirectly about the importance of prioritizing people. Almost all of them did, including Jodie McLean, the CEO of EDENS, a real estate firm with more than $6.5 billion in assets. And Jodie pointed out that prioritizing people doesn't mean that you always agree with them.

Just before Jodie joined me for our interview, she was in a meeting with several members of her team and they were trying to solve what she described as a "pretty big problem." It was a diverse group—so diverse, in fact, that they didn't all see eye to eye, but this was exactly the type of meeting Jodie thrives in.

"I think that is fantastic," she told me. "I'm really comfortable in that environment. I love harmonious discord."

Jodie prioritizes people by promoting a culture at EDENS where it's okay to have different opinions and disagreements over how to solve the firm's challenges. Her role, she said, is to make sure that culture maintains a harmonious spirit so that discord leads to better decisions, not hostilities. That only happens, she said, if she values people and if the people around her value people.

For Jodie, it's as simple as this: Be kind.

"I think this gets lost a lot of the time, but one of the most underrated values of leadership is kindness," she told me. "I think our world needs more kindness. You can be decisive.

You can be open and honest. You can have harmonious discord. But in business, I think we should be leading with kindness. And it's more important now than ever."

Kindness, of course, is displayed in the context of relationships and community. Those don't just exist inside the walls of EDENS but also in its portfolio of more than a hundred open-air retail and mixed-use developments across the country. And Jodie's passion for kindness shapes the companies approach to all of those developments, she said.

With the growth of omni-channel shopping, Jodie recognized the need to rethink EDENS role in the retail industry. They could reinvent themselves as a tech company and emphasize online transactional retail, or they could stay in the physical world but place a higher value and emphasis on humanity and community.

They chose the latter. In fact, they created a new purpose statement for EDENS—"to enrich community through human engagement"—and it's something Jodie has grown even more passionate about in the aftermath of the pandemic.

She cares about the financial success of EDENS, of course, but she's also driven by the "social impact that we make every day for fifteen million people and that we are building places where people can emotionally connect with other human beings."

In our post-pandemic, hyper-digital world, Jodie sees an epidemic of "isolation, loneliness, and depression" and believes EDENS is helping solve it by developing brick-and-mortar projects that intentionally help people connect with each other and feel like they are part of a community.

EDENS, in fact, measures its success on four key performance indicators—employee engagement, retailer productivity, total shareholder return, and a set of community impact statistics on health, crime, education, and opportunities around their developments.

It's an endless loop, she said, because having a positive impact on communities helps produce higher employee engagement scores, which leads to success for their retail partners and shareholders as well as a positive impact on communities.

"Our people want to be paid fairly," she said, "but that's not enough. What really drives them is the impact that they can make every day on human lives—people in most cases that they'll never know."

With that type of priority on people and an infusion of kindness, Jodie and her team can effectively use harmonious discord to sort through myriad ideas, perspectives, and opinions based on a variety of divergent backgrounds. Then they can skip the hostilities and celebrate their results.

PRIORITIZING KINDNESS

Susan Stewart, the CEO of SWBC Mortgage in San Antonio, entered the mortgage business in the 1980s, a time when turnover rates in the industry were high and kindness often seemed in short supply.

"There was always a lot of cyclical hiring and firing, and like in any environment, people aren't always kind to one another," she told me. "Kindness is not required in the business world a lot of the time. Smart and hardworking, yes. But kind, not so much."

Susan, however, wants kindness to be a priority at SWBC Mortgage, which has licensed loan officers in forty states and is widely considered one of the top mortgage lenders in the United States. So she not only prioritized kindness in her personal approach to leadership, but it's something she looks for when hiring, building teams, and addressing personnel issues.

"I can teach somebody the business," she told me, "but I haven't been successful teaching people to be nice. And I'm not interested in having people work together who don't care about one another and who create an unkind environment. I used to tell people all the time, 'I'm not gonna fire you for making a mistake. But if you're really crummy to a bunch of people, I will fire you because we don't have that here.'"

That can sound a bit idealistic, but Susan has found that kindness spreads and becomes part of your culture if she lives it as a leader, requires it from others, and finds the right people for her teams.

"That's what your organization becomes," she said. "People caring about each other, people looking out for each other, doing something when somebody's having a hard time. And that is very much our culture in the mortgage company here."

Susan knows everyone isn't going to be nice all the time, and that's okay. But over the years she's learned from experience about the value of kindness. And, interestingly, that value has grown parallel to her empathy for others.

"When you're leading a group of people, it's really important that you think about the people and the example you're setting, but also how you're treating them," she said. "And so I think empathy has helped me. We have a track record of people not leaving this company very often, and I don't think that's a special skill set I have. Business is hard. The mortgage business is hard. But the mortgage business is not a lot more difficult than other businesses. Sometimes it's great; sometimes it's terrible. But if you work in an environment where you feel like people care about you and respect you, it doesn't get better than that. We can execute all day long. Execution's not an issue."

Prioritizing people is the issue.

DREAM CATCHERS

▷ Putting empathy into practice is a critical component to the principle of prioritizing people. When we prioritize empathy, we nurture related skills like concern and compassion for others.

▷ Getting to know people and appreciating their stories and what matters to them builds trust and respect in those relationships.

▷ Just because you have different views from someone doesn't mean those differences are driven by bias.

▷ Empathy is a choice.

▷ All relational experiences, good or bad, are formative. You can always learn something of value.

▷ The better you get to know people and understand things like their communication style or the baggage in their background, the more successfully you can build a healthy relationship and support them in their goals for life.

▷ Kindness is an underrated value of leadership. Prioritizing kindness makes you a better leader, and prioritizing it in your organizational culture helps you build a more successful company.

QUESTIONS

1. In what relationships might you work harder to develop more empathy by learning more about the other person's background and life circumstances?
2. How comfortable are you with harmonious discord?

PRINCIPLE 11

GIVE GENEROUSLY

Priscilla Almodovar was in the middle of a three-year tenure as president and CEO of Enterprise Community Partners when the national social enterprise announced a new initiative that perfectly reflects the impact she's tried to make throughout her professional career.

Enterprise, which focuses on increasing the number of affordable rental homes in America, partnered with Morgan Stanley in 2021 to create the Disaster Recovery Accelerator Fund that helps the owners of multifamily rental properties make repairs more quickly after damage caused by a natural disaster.

Rather than waiting nearly two years on relief funding from the US government, qualified property owners can tap into the fund, which was seeded by Morgan Stanley with $25 million, start making repairs, and get tenants back in their homes much sooner. They pay only the interest on the three-year loan while using government relief funds, when they finally arrive, to pay back the principal.

The initiative is the type of public-private partnership Priscilla has cultivated throughout her career, which has included work in the private sector, with the government, and with nonprofits. And now as president and CEO of Fannie Mae, the government-sponsored mortgage company that's number twenty-eight on the Fortune 500 list, she continues to combine her lifelong appreciation for affordable housing with her gifts and passions for finance.

"One thing I've discovered about myself is that I'm very finance-oriented," Priscilla told me. "And at Enterprise, I learned I could take my finance experience and do good. Enterprise was that rare organization that was at the intersection of public policy, so they understood all the FEMA and HUD programs and financing because they have partners like Morgan Stanley, JPMorgan, and Goldman Sachs that provide capital. It was basically bridge capital."

Doing good was an incredibly strong theme in my interviews, validating that giving generously is an indispensable principle for leaders. It's not just something you do once you attain a level of success; it's essential to the process of creating a successful life story.

This plays out in a variety of ways. All of the leaders I interviewed sit on corporate and nonprofit boards and give their time and money to worthwhile causes. It's part of who they are.

Diane Batayeh, the CEO of Detroit-based Village Green, for instance, established a personal family foundation to benefit Detroit inner-city education, homelessness, and ovarian cancer research. Village Green's corporate philanthropy, meanwhile, includes partnerships with Ronald McDonald House Charities, Animal Placement Bureau, Move for Hunger, and various other environmental nonprofits, including One Tree Planted and Planet Water Foundation.

"Giving back is a central theme in my life," she told me. "I strongly believe that the more you have, the more responsibility you have to give back. That upward spiral of sharing your good fortune leads to more good fortune in immeasurable ways."

Connie Moore, former CEO of BRE Properties, calls it her "personal flag," a metaphor she came up with at BRE to help people think about and focus on the deeper reasons for why their work mattered.

"My personal flag is that I want to make a lot of money," she said. "But it's not about making the money. It's about giving an endowment to San Jose State. It's about supporting family members who need help. It's not about me buying bigger houses, more cars, or that kind of stuff. It's about what I can do with the money."

Every leader I interviewed had personal flags that involved giving generously.

David Kong, the former president and CEO of BWH Hotel Group, is founder and principle of DEI Advisors, a nonprofit that supports the success of next-generation minority leaders in the hotel industry.

And Mit Shah, CEO of Noble Investment Group, endowed the Bharat Shah Leadership Speaker Series at Georgia State in honor of his father. The program brings in high-profile leaders—from CEOs like Mark Hoplamazian of Hyatt and the late Arne Sorenson of Marriott to NBA greats like Vince Carter and Grant Hill—to the university's school of hospitality for candid conversations about their journey.

Many of the leaders I interviewed would say that their work also takes a form of giving generously, because they are using their gifts and talents to pursue goals that help people and communities. That's certainly the case for Priscilla, who sees her career in affordable housing as a calling that was cultivated by her parents and the community in which she was raised.

Priscilla's parents both came to New York from Puerto Rico as teenagers in the 1950s. They met, married, and started a family in Brooklyn, so Priscilla, the middle of three children, spent the first four years of her life living in a rented apartment in a four-story walk-up nestled in a tightly knit Puerto Rican neighborhood.

"The first few years of my life, I thought everyone was Puerto Rican," Priscilla told me. "I really did. It was an amazing community. We had great public schools. I lived right next to Sunset Park. My doctor's office was like two blocks away. Our church was nearby. So within a ten-block radius, I had this amazing community."

Her parents bought their first home in Brooklyn when Priscilla was five and moved the family to Long Island—where she discovered that everyone, in fact, was not Puerto Rican—when she was thirteen. She graduated from high school and left for college when she was only sixteen but never forgot that sense of community she experienced while growing up.

"I still remember as a five-year-old, when my parents saved to buy their first home and that home changed the trajectory of our life," Priscilla said during a panel discussion in 2023. "I'm exhibit A of the American Dream. That home is how they paid for college for three kids…. Housing is something that's very personal, and that's what Fannie Mae does, so it's a real privilege."[1]

After earning an undergraduate degree in economics at Hofstra and a law degree from Columbia, Priscilla joined the prestigious White & Case law firm, where she spent fourteen years and became a partner while specializing in international work.

When she and her husband started their family, however, she decided to look for new career options that would allow her to spend less time traveling away from home. She ran the New York State Housing Finance Agency for three years, then spent nine years in real estate–related roles for JPMorgan Chase and three years with Enterprise before taking the helm at Fannie Mae late in 2022.

"I've been very fortunate in that my work is no longer a job," Priscilla said. "It really is a calling. I've been able to create this career and do something that I just really love."

Priscilla, in fact, was willing to take substantial pay cuts to run Enterprise and Fannie Mae so that she could do purpose-driven work she enjoyed and knew would have a positive impact on society. It was her way of giving back.

---

1   Michele Cantos, "Fannie Mae's First Latina CEO on Housing, Mortgages and Latino Unity," *Hispanic Executive*, July 18, 2023, https://hispanicexecutive.com/fannie-maes-first-latina-ceo-on-housing-mortgages-and-latino-unity/.

"I've always lived modestly compared to where I could live," she told me. "Money's not my only motivator. It sounds corny, but I want to have impact and still do finance."

As CEO of Fannie Mae, which had more than $4.1 trillion in assets and annual revenues of $29.7 billion as of December 31, 2022, Priscilla oversees a company that's involved in one in four mortgages in the United States.

"Home ownership is still the number one way households build wealth in this country," she said. "I believe in the story. I am Exhibit A of what Fannie Mae is all about."

DOING WELL BY DOING GOOD

Patricia Will, the founder of Belmont Village Senior Living, also sees her industry—a combination of senior housing and health care—as a conduit for making a positive impact on society. But this career wasn't the fulfillment of a lifelong dream.

"I didn't figure it out right off the bat," Patricia told me. "Belmont is my second career."

Patricia spent the early part of her journey working for Mischer Development, where she developed several million square feet of commercial and medical projects for the legendary Houston-based firm. Then, like many entrepreneurs, Patricia spotted a societal need and realized she had the skills and experiences to address it by starting a business.

The need was for senior housing communities that included help with health-care needs, and she noticed it in the early 1990s when her mother-in-law began going through the early stages of dementia. Patricia and her husband looked at options for support and care but found them lacking.

With her background in real estate, she and her partners agreed to develop a seniors' housing community near the medical center in Houston, but they couldn't find anyone to operate it in the way they were envisioning.

"So we took out a blank sheet of paper and decided we would create an operating company," she said.

That company became Belmont, which now operates more than thirty communities in the United States, as well as one in Mexico City. It offers options for assisted living, memory care, personal care, and independent living that can include around-the-clock licensed nurses, medication and diabetes management, and professional therapy services.

"As I look at my career and ask myself why I am still doing this, the answer is that it's very rare and special to be in an industry where you do well by doing good," Patricia told me. "The intangible reward of getting what you get by giving back in your profession, as opposed to apart from your profession and in charitable pursuits, is really special."

THE POWER OF SPONSORSHIPS

Tom Baltimore, the chairman and CEO of Park Hotels & Resorts, is a man who exudes self-confidence, and he never doubted that he could handle the academic work when he was at the University of Virginia. But that doesn't mean he had a worry-free life in college.

"My biggest fear as an undergrad was that somebody would show up with a bill, because I had no safety net," he said. "My anxiety was around the financial cost. I knew I could do the work."[2]

Tom grew up in a family that worked hard but didn't have much money. His father founded a church and was a pastor for most of his career; his mother worked part-time while raising Tom and his four siblings. So Tom has always felt a strong conviction about giving back, especially to help students.

Tom and his wife, Hilary, established and support a variety of endowed scholarships and fellowships for minority students, including the Sylvia V. Terry Scholarship, which

---

2   McGregor McCance, "Tom Baltimore: An Alum's Journey from Humble Beginnings to Corporate CEO," *UVAToday*, September 14, 2022, https://news.virginia.edu/content/tom-baltimore-alums-journey-humble-beginnings-corporate-ceo.

honors a former assistant dean of admission at UVA. When Tom transferred to Virginia in the early 1980s after one year at Baldwin Wallace in Ohio, Terry became a mentor who helped him make the transition.

They also support the Jefferson Scholars Foundation, which provides full scholarships to UVA undergraduate students and a fellowship specifically for MBA students in UVA's Darden School of Business.

But Tom's approach to giving isn't just through donation or by serving on boards at the University of Virginia and within the hospitality industry. He also has given guest lectures at Darden for more than a decade, and one of the things he teaches is something he benefited from and practiced throughout his career—mentoring and sponsorships.

Tom has benefited from mentors and been a mentor (see Principle 3), but he also advocates for taking mentoring to another level by going beyond giving advice and investing more intentionally in someone's career. Sponsors, he said, are the gatekeepers in an organization who can create opportunities, increase responsibility, and give stretch assignments that are key to career development.

This type of giving involves time to get to know people and a willingness to take risks to help them advance.

"I love pushing people out of their comfort zone," Tom said. "You can see that they have more talent than they even see themselves. I enjoy watching them grow and excel, watching a team succeed by itself."[3]

GIVE TO YOUR FAMILY

Sometimes it's worth remembering that charity begins at home, and that starts by giving generously to your family.

---

3   McGregor McCance, "Tom Baltimore: An Alum's Journey from Humble Beginnings to Corporate CEO," *UVAToday*, September 14, 2022, https://news.virginia.edu/content/tom-baltimore-alums-journey-humble-beginnings-corporate-ceo.

Several leaders I interviewed, especially the women, spoke about the challenges to balance their careers with their commitment to their families, and they consistently talked about the importance of prioritizing their time.

Perhaps my favorite anecdote about giving quality time to family came from Jodie McLean, the CEO of the real estate development firm EDENS and a mother of four children.

"I had this wonderful routine with my son," she told me. "We'd eat dinner at this little table, and I'd light a candle. It didn't matter if we were eating Chick-fil-A, we'd eat on our dishes and linen napkins. And then we'd read books. He'd go to bed, and I'd sit back at my desk and I'd work."

OPENING DOORS

One of the ways many leaders give back is by getting involved in industry organizations. This can have multiple benefits, especially for younger leaders. They get to meet other people in their industries, so their network expands. And they get to serve in areas that are connected to their interests. Then with time and experience comes added responsibilities and greater impact within these organizations, so there are opportunities to shape the future and how business is done.

Debra Still, for instance, was president and CEO for eighteen years and now is vice chair of Pulte Financial Services, which includes Pulte Mortgage, PGP Title, and PCIC Insurance. But she's also been active in the Mortgage Bankers Association (MBA) for nearly two decades, serving on its board since 2012 and as its chair in 2013. She also has chaired the MBA's residential board of governors, served on its strategic planning committee, was chair of its strategic task force, and was a member of its loan origination task force, affordable housing committee, and secondary and capital markets committee.

Debra estimated that she traveled around eighty-five thousand miles the year she was the MBA chair, because she was essentially working two full-time jobs.

"I loved every second of it," she said. "And the executive team at Pulte Financial Services was so supportive of my chairmanship, stepping up and running our company in a way that it hadn't had to before. I couldn't have done it without the strength of our leadership team."

Debra testified before Congress on behalf of the industry, but one of her most lasting contributions was sparked by something that others had to point out to her.

"At the end of my first board meeting as chair at MBA, three male board members came up to me and said, 'Deb, this is a travesty. You are the only female in the room,'" she said. "I hadn't even noticed because I was so used to that environment."

One of them happened to be the only Hispanic person in the room. Another was the only Black person in the room.

"So I chartered the MBA Diversity Board," Debra said. "We committed to identifying our diverse leaders across the country and making sure that all of our future panels had diversity on the stage. And we also made a commitment to diversifying our board of directors. It took three or four years to get traction, but it all started because of their bold observation after that first board meeting. I was so used to being the only female in the room that I hadn't even noticed. They had. It was a powerful moment of both thought and action that has led to the increasing diversity of our industry."

Debra's work with MBA, however, hasn't been limited to the people within her industry. On the day we spoke, she had already been hard at work on behalf of the MBA Opens Doors Foundation, which provides families with mortgage and rental assistance so they can stay in their homes when their critically ill or injured children are undergoing treatment.

"We do an annual fundraising campaign," she told me. "I think we've raised $1.8 million since eight o'clock this morning. I send out an email and throughout the day everybody chimes in—about two hundred CEOs from real estate finance all over the country. They pledge personally as well as make corporate donations. 2023 has been a pretty tough year for our industry, but many leaders generously stepped up, and many others did what they could. We ultimately raised $2.8 million from an industry that gives from the heart. That is what giving is all about—supporting others in a time of need."

DREAM CATCHERS

▷ Giving generously isn't something you do once you become successful; it is an indispensable principle that leads to success.

▷ The more you have, the more responsibility you have to give back.

▷ There are many ways to give generously—with your time, your energy, your expertise, your money, or whatever else of value you have.

▷ Your work itself can become a form of generous giving when what you do for a living adds value to the lives of people.

▷ Giving generously is a form of honoring those who generously gave to support your success.

▷ Generous giving includes giving generously to your family, friends, and others you love, as well as by getting involved in organizations that support the industry in which you work.

QUESTIONS

1. What causes do you support in a way that costs you something?
2. In what ways have generous givers had a positive impact on your life?
3. Who are you giving generously to as a mentor or sponsor?

Part III

A LITTLE LAGNIAPPE

Eric Blehm, the author of *Fearless*, was asked in an interview if there were any interesting stories that didn't make it into the final version of his 2012 biography of Navy SEAL Adam Brown.

There were, and he shared one that illustrated the type of courage Brown would display throughout much of his life.

Brown and his older brother were crossing an open field as children, Blehm said, when a vicious dog began pursuing them. Brown, only six years old at the time, was slower than the dog and slower than his eleven-year-old brother. The odds were against him until he turned, stood his ground, and, with the baseball bat he was carrying, fought off the dog (who was stunned but otherwise not injured).[1]

How could that story not make it into the book?!

It's not unusual, of course. Not every story fits the narrative, and therefore some perfectly useful and interesting content doesn't end up on the pages. In this case, Blehm used plenty of other stories that made a similar point, most of which showed Brown's instinctive willingness to protect others and not just himself.

The interviews for this book, as I've mentioned, yielded far more content than could be used. I left out some stories because I didn't want to overdo a point that already had been

1   Eric Blehm, "Interview: Eric Blehm on *Fearless*," ChristianAudio, May 21, 2012, audio, https://christianaudio.com/interview-eric-blehm-on-fearless-audiobook-download.

made, and others were off topic from my outline. But a few of them were just too good for me not to share, so I decided to offer what I'll call a "lagniappe" chapter.

Folks in the New Orleans area use that Cajun-French term to describe something good they get that's free and "a little extra" from what was expected or due.

So enjoy some lagniappe.

TOUGH LOVE

Gil Hill played a memorable supporting role in the 1980s *Beverly Hills Cop* film series that starred Eddie Murphy. Hill wasn't a professional actor. He was a sergeant for the Detroit police department, and he was recruited to play Murphy's outspoken and sometimes foul-mouthed boss—a deputy police chief in Detroit.

He also coached Daryl Carter's youth basketball team, and he sometimes coached with the same tough-love approach as the movie character he portrayed.

Here's an example as Daryl recalled it.

"Carter, bring your butt over here," Hill said during one practice. "There are two problems when you catch the ball in the paint."

"Yes, sir," Daryl replied.

"One, you only have one effing move," Hill went on.

"Yes, sir," Daryl said. "What's the second thing?"

"The move sucks."

As Daryl pointed out, you no longer coach kids that way. But he didn't feel bullied, he said. He just went to work on a move that didn't suck, and he eventually earned a scholarship to play at the University of Michigan.

THE STAGES OF YOUR DREAMS

It's been said that there are three stages of career development: One, I want to be in the meeting. Two, I want to run the meeting. Three, I want to avoid meetings.

That rings true, but it's not quite as helpful as the deeper descriptions I got from a few leaders about the stages they see when it comes to career development.

David Kong, for instance, talked about the individual contributor stage, the team leader stage, and the visionary leader stage.

The individual contributor stage is when you are starting out and you really have to prove your worth.

"You have to show you are a knowledgeable person—the person others go to for any kind of extra work or difficult task," David said. "You are the go-to person."

That leads to more responsibilities as a team leader.

"And that's when you get to the art of building a team—finding people who are smarter and more knowledgeable than you, and feeling comfortable about letting go and empowering them to achieve success," he said. "At the same time, you're comfortable in holding people accountable in a respectful way. And when you can do that, then you're proving yourself as a successful team leader."

In the next stage, you become a visionary leader.

"And to achieve that," David said, "you have to have intellectual curiosity. You have to be well read, well informed, be in tune with your environment, develop the ability to see the general direction of everything, and be able to project the future. In other words, you need strategic visioning skills. But above all, you have to have the courage to challenge your status quo. And you have to have the courage to pursue your vision, because it's going to be really difficult to convince people to let go of the familiar."

Jodie McLean, meanwhile, has seen her career unfold in chapters.

The first she calls the "sponge" chapter when she said yes to just about every opportunity and wasn't scared to risk failure to learn as much as possible. After going a mile wide and an inch deep, she realized she needed to gain expertise in one field. During that chapter, she gained the confidence in herself that led to her next chapter: thought leadership. She was better equipped to look beyond the immediate needs of the day, see emerging trends, and develop new ideas for her business.

DON'T SLEEP ON TALENT

It's not unusual for real estate investment companies to have diversity when it comes to service or property management jobs, Daryl Carter told me. "But very few times are those people considered for acquisitions, asset management, or some of the other wealth-creation positions in real estate firms," he said.

Leaders and managers, he said, need to be more proactive at providing those opportunities.

"We've been very intentional at Avanath about taking people who are stars and moving them to a position where they can get a higher wealth-creation opportunity," he said.

Too often, however, leaders fail to recognize the potential in would-be stars.

Daryl tells the story of a young analyst at a large investment firm who wanted to get into sales, marketing, and acquisitions. He had a degree from Brown University and five years of professional experience, but the company's CEO told the analyst he needed an MBA. So he went to an Ivy League school and got one. The CEO still wasn't sure the analyst would do well in sales, so he called Daryl.

"I have a young, talented African American who wants to do the sales side," he said, as Daryl recalled the conversation.

"I don't know whether he can cut it, but I know you could evaluate whether he can."

Daryl agreed to meet with the man, found him incredibly talented, and asked what he wanted to do in his career.

"He was interested in acquisitions, and I told him I had an acquisitions position," Daryl said. "I made him an offer and hired him on the spot."

The CEO, as you might expect, was surprised. He wanted Daryl to talk to the man, not hire him.

"He didn't want to talk," Daryl said. "He wanted a job, and if they weren't smart enough to hire him, I would."

That hire now is a senior vice president at Avanath and among several star performers on Daryl's team who came largely because some other company wasn't willing to take a risk on them.

SURVIVING A FALL

It was 1995, and Chris Howard was practicing a Cuban eight—an aerobatic maneuver that would take his air force training jet through three-quarters of a normal loop, add a half roll, then three-quarters of another normal loop and another half roll before pulling out of the dive and returning to level flight.

It didn't go well. There were multiple issues, not all of which were caused by Chris. The aircraft got into what he said was a "Mach tuck" and the nose was too low for Chris to recover and stabilize the aircraft. He inadvertently hit a "trim tab," adding to his difficulty in properly controlling his speed, and there was nothing he could do to keep the plane from going down.

"I had to bail out," he told me. "I won't go into the details, but I almost died in this plane crash."

For Chris, who now is executive vice president and COO of Arizona State University, it became an enduring life lesson on several levels.

Chris had been the starting running back for the Air Force Academy football team, class president, a cadet group commander, an Academic All-American, and a Rhodes Scholar. But he realized his impressive string of successes as a scholar, an athlete, and an air force cadet didn't guarantee him success in whatever he might do next.

"When you have success early on and people start building you up, there's a risk that you can fall in love with your résumé," he told me. "It's not that you think you are infallible but just that things are always going to go your way."

The plane crash caused Chris to acknowledge that he was human and made mistakes, but it also left him with choices of how to respond. That response, he would learn, would be shaped by who he was but also by who was with him.

"Shame is a terrible thing," Chris told me. "I was ashamed of a mistake that I had made. I didn't want to call my friends. I didn't want to interact. And then when I came out of surgery, there was my best friend from the Air Force Academy—a Black guy who, incidentally, just recently retired as a two-star general. He had flown to San Antonio and got into the recovery room somehow. He was sitting there across from me, and I thought I was hallucinating. And he's like, 'I'm here for you.' So the people supporting me after the accident was pretty phenomenal."

Chris recovered from his injuries, including major knee surgery. The investigation into the accident, meanwhile, revealed his mistakes contributed to the crash, but it also found mistakes were made in the way he had been trained. He was reinstated, and he became a helicopter pilot and intelligence officer who was awarded several medals, including a Bronze Star for his service in Afghanistan.

"There have been some really gritty low moments that I've been able to overcome that have made me better," he said. "That's probably the one that's the most evident. In some ways, it was the best thing that happened to me and the worst thing that happened to me at the same time. To get over that helped make me the man I am."

It gave him perspective and a reservoir of confidence that he could overcome other challenges and setbacks in life.

"If you can almost die in a plane crash, then get back in the cockpit, do the same maneuver you almost died in, and continue to serve," he told himself, "well, brother, you've got something on the ball. And it's not because you're a NASA rocket scientist. It's just because you have a level of toughness that maybe came from your kinfolk and your ancestors."

THE PATH FORWARD

My interviews with the twenty-four leaders featured throughout this book produced some amazing stories. And while interesting stories are great—and I thought there were plenty worth sharing at our next dinner party—it's the transferable life lessons that matter most. Those provide the best practices we can use each day to grow personally and professionally. They are the extractable superpowers from the principles that emerged in the stories.

As you might have noticed, the eleven principles often overlapped. They don't exist in a vacuum. They feed each other and feed off each other, so the more we develop them simultaneously, the greater sum of the parts.

For instance, the first principle we looked at was that character counts and the last principle was to give generously. Those are unique and distinct concepts, but I don't think it was coincidental that both involve "doing good."

The intention to do good in business, as we learned from Lynn Katzmann's passion for improving the world through Juniper Communities, is born of important character traits such as charity and service. And when we have "doing good" ingrained in our character, we give generously, as we saw in the story of Patricia Will and Belmont Village.

Likewise, character is at the heart of other types of generous giving, not just as part of our work but in all areas of life—as we learned from, well, from everyone I interviewed.

Our character—hard work, integrity, humility, and respect for others, for instance—also plays a role in our self-confidence, which gives us the courage to ask *why not* us when opportunities present themselves and to persevere when we get knocked down or when the would-be saboteurs around us try to get us to settle for less than our potential.

And when we develop and display strength of character, people notice and want to help—people who become our champions.

Think about the story of how a young Daryl Carter dealt with the racist client. There are many different ways to handle difficult situations like the one he faced, so what Daryl did wasn't necessarily a prescription for every circumstance. But Daryl didn't blow up in anger and let his emotions lead his responses. He maintained his self-respect. And he acted with class and dignity. Those aspects of his character are prescriptions that work for anyone, at any time, in any situation. And they play a key role in earning trust and respect from those around you.

On the other hand, if we consistently lie, take shortcuts, and act like jerks, the leaders who could help aren't likely to risk their reputation on us—and, as Susan Stewart pointed out, they might even send us in search of employment elsewhere.

Dedication to our work, meanwhile, was a principle on its own, and it takes that type of commitment to develop the other principles. They don't just happen. And the leaders I interviewed were nothing if not proactive in working hard to grow personally and professionally. They strategically invested in long hours, not just for the benefit of their organizations but for self-improvement (the principle of living to learn).

Think about Leslie Hale and Jodie McLean, for example, who both arranged their work schedules so they could spend a few minutes each week one-on-one picking the brains of their mentors. They were doing the hard work that resulted in learning the things that helped them become who they are as leaders.

If we love what we do and are passionate about our work, we find our work worth the effort. Gratitude, which results in generous giving, then flows naturally from our work. A love for our work motivates us not only to commit to our work but to get back up when we are knocked down, to figure out how to play the hand we are dealt rather than complaining about it, and to pursue our aspirations rather than settling.

We focus more on what we are doing and what needs to be done and less on the fact that there are barriers in our way.

Exposing ourselves to new ideas and learning new things, meanwhile, helps us discover ways to apply the passions we have and discover new passions. Think about leaders like Amy Price, Leslie Hale, and Alice Carr, who took very different paths by doing things that interested them and discovered how to mix their passions with their skills to create incredible careers.

In all of these examples, and many others you no doubt noticed along the way, the principles wove together to form a tight net that supports success.

These principles come more easily to some than others. We might be born with curiosity, a love for helping people, or a strong desire to do whatever it takes to finish a job we've started. And maybe we've had the benefit of extraordinary families that nurtured these principles in us when we were growing up. Certainly one of the most common parts of the stories I heard from leaders was their gratitude for their parents, grandparents, and other family members.

Where does that leave you, however, if you grew up in a dysfunctional family or if, for whatever reason, some or all of these principles seem as alien to you as a language spoken on a distant planet?

What I believe, and what was confirmed to me throughout these interviews, is that the principles it takes to succeed as leaders are ideals anyone can pursue and develop, regardless of their starting point.

Living Beyond Your Dreams, in other words, is a process, not a destination. And every experience throughout the process adds value to the next phase of the journey.

"People often look at the end result," Leslie Hale told me. "They don't really appreciate the journey and the learning curve and the challenges that we face. Whether it's internal or external, they don't go away. They stay with you. You just have to learn to power through them, you know? You have to not let it stop you."

Everyone's background is unique. The baggage and the privileges of your experiences are distinctively yours. So are your skills and talents. And so are the circumstances you face. Yet there is truly nothing new under the sun. You have the benefit of learning from others who are enough like you and who have faced similar trials and challenges to the ones you face.

You might not do exactly what they did or what they would do, but you can apply the same principles that led to their decisions, actions, and outcomes. If you put forth the effort, commit to honorable character, and open yourself to help, then others will come along to lend a hand. And day by day, you will move toward places you never imagined possible. You will live beyond your dreams.

ACKNOWLEDGMENTS

All books are team efforts, and this one is no different. This project never would have come to life without the invaluable contributions of the people who provided their support and expertise.

I want to again acknowledge my wife, Penny, for seeing the value of the project, agreeing to sacrifice some of our time together so that I could work on it, and lending her opinions and insights on the vision and execution.

I also want to thank my collaborator, Stephen Caldwell, whose literary style has made our powerful message a joy to read; my team, principally Kim Chantelois and Kerri Horton, who provided countless hours of research and support; and the team at Post Hill Press.

Finally, this book would not have been possible without the twenty-four leaders who were interviewed for their experiences and insights: Priscilla Almodovar, Tom Baltimore, Diane Batayeh, Alice Carr, Daryl Carter, Lili Dunn, Tammy Fischer, Leslie Hale, Chris Howard, Lynne Katzmann, Angela Kleiman, David Kong, Gerry Lopez, Jodie W. McLean, Connie Moore, Clarence Otis, Denny Marie Post, Mary Hogan Preusse, Amy Price, Sumit Roy, Mit Shah, Susan Stewart, Debra Still, and Patricia Will.

ABOUT THE AUTHOR

William J. Ferguson serves as co-chairman and chief executive officer of Ferguson Partners. Mr. Ferguson conducts senior management recruiting assignments, with a specialization in president and chief executive officer searches and recruiting assignments for boards of trustees and directors. He also conducts CEO succession planning assignments and facilitates public company board assessments and senior management assessments.

In 2022, Mr. Ferguson launched The Ferguson Centers for Leadership Excellence (CLE) Foundation. The foundation's program helps racially and ethnically diverse students by offering tuition and financial assistance, mentoring and coaching, and the opportunity to earn undergraduate degrees and secure promising careers in real estate and related sectors. Mr. Ferguson and his spouse, Penny Ferguson, are committed to creating an ecosystem of inclusion, opportunity, and justice for future generations.

Before founding Ferguson Partners, Mr. Ferguson was a managing director with one of the leading international executive recruiting consultants. There he co-managed the firm's national real estate practice. Prior to focusing on real estate, Mr. Ferguson worked for General Mills in Minneapolis in strategic marketing. He holds a bachelor's degree from Harvard University, where he was a member of Phi Beta Kappa, and an MBA in marketing from the Wharton Graduate School of Business.

Mr. Ferguson also serves as executive-in-residence for New York University's C. H. Chen Institute for Global Real Estate Finance and as fellow for the University of Virginia's Frank Batten School of Leadership and Public Policy.